T0208010

ATTITUDES OF STUDENTS WITH LEARNING DISABILITIES TOWARD PARTICIPATION IN PHYSICAL EDUCATION:

A TEACHERS' PERSPECTIVE - QUALITATIVE EXAMINATION

ELLIE ABDI

authorHOUSE

AuthorHouse™
1663 Liberty Drive
Bloomington, IN 47403
www.authorhouse.com
Phone: 1 (800) 839-8640

Published by AuthorHouse 10/08/2019

ISBN: 978-1-7283-3100-3 (sc)
ISBN: 978-1-7283-3099-0 (e)

Contents

List of Tables

Abstract

Many researchers have confirmed that students with disabilities engage in significantly less physical activity than their nondisabled peers in physical education class. One of the elements that influences student participation in physical education class is attitude, and there is a gap in the literature with respect to investigating the attitudes of students with learning disabilities, emotional/behavioral disabilities, or attention difficulties. While there is research indicating lack of participation in physical education class, there is limited research on how teachers perceive and assist students to participate in physical education.

The purpose of this qualitative case study was to understand the perceptions of physical education teachers and their experiences with learning disabled students in their classes. More specifically, this research filled the gap in the literature about attitudes that learning disabled students have about physical education in school. Using teachers' perceptions, this study was designed to inform future practice related to teaching of physical education to students with learning disabilities. Understanding the perspectives of teachers is crucial in educational research. Suggested strategies to increase physical activity are needed to guide physical educators in teaching of students with learning disabilities. Teachers' perceptions of these students' attitudes toward and participation in physical education were assessed through semi-structured interviews of teachers. The population consisted of 10 physical education teachers assigned to PreK-12 physical education classes in a district in Northeast of the United States participated in this study. Semi-structured interviews contained of 10 questions guided the researcher in answering the research questions. Using teachers' perceptions and suggested strategies, this study was designed to assist and inform future practice related to teaching of physical education to students with learning disabilities.

Interview data were collected to examine factors influencing attitudes toward physical activity during physical education and analyzed through hand coding. Key finding of the study extracted from the interviews revealed seven major dimensions:

(a) enjoyment, (b) usefulness, (c) inclusion, (d) co-education, (e) limited lack of physical education, (f) factors in lack of physical education, and (g) suggestions and experiences. Education staff have meaningful jurisdiction throughout all these factors influencing students' attitudes toward physical education. Considerations of known factors influencing the attitudes of students with learning disabilities toward physical education may result in progressive consequences.

Recommendations for practice included: (a) offering encouragement and propose motivation, (b) co-education practices, (c) considering lessons which are intensely structured, and (d) educate all students in inclusion or self-contained gymnasiums. Recommendations for future research included: (a) research considering children with disability as sample size and (b) inconsistent with finding of this research study, lack of physical education for students with disabilities need to be explore further.

Acknowledgements

This dissertation is dedicated to my husband Hooshmand Victor whom without his support survival through this process was impossible, he neither lost faith nor doubted me. And to my own children, Joshua and Jacob who are the reasons behind my profession. I hope someday they realize that some journeys worth pursuing.

Many thanks to my chair Dr. Candace Adams, the thoughtful comments and insights provided, no doubt helped me to improve and I am forever grateful for her confidence in me. To my committee member Dr. Meena Clowes who was able to make the impossible a reality and to my dissertation coach Dr. Ferguson, this was unfeasible without the furnished aid. To my father Professor G. Husien Dehbozorgi and my mother Ms. Zari Setayesh both educators who instilled the love of knowledge in me. And to my sister Avid Bozorgi for her ongoing support.

Thanks to my students whose beautiful faces encouraged me every day to learn. To participant district and principals, success through this process was impossible without their contributions. To participated teachers, I was so fortunate to be surrounded with such competent professionals for giving the time and resources. The input may someday shape policies and approaches toward implanting positive outlooks in young people with learning disabilities toward physical activity in physical education.

From a little girl entering kindergarten at Hadaf grammar school in Tehran many years ago to achieving the highest academic degree, I thank everyone who had a part in my educational life.

Chapter 1

Introduction

Poor lifestyle behaviors, including suboptimal diet, physical inactivity, and tobacco use are leading causes of preventable diseases globally (Mozaffarian, Afshin, Benowitz, Bittner, Daniels, Franchand, & Zakai, 2012).The foundation for healthy lifestyle behaviors begin in childhood (Kelly, Melnyk, Jacobson & O'Haver, 2011). Nevertheless, unhealthy lifestyle behaviors have been identified as a problem amongst students under the age of 18 (Dodd, Al-Nakeeb, Nevill & Forshaw, 2010).

The importance of continued engagement in physical activity and usefulness of physical education have been highlighted in recent research for children. Findings demonstrate the positive effects of exercise on physical, mental, and emotional health (Center for Disease Control and Prevention [cdc], 2011; Lai, Costigan, Morgan, Lubans, Stodden, Salmon& Barnett, 2014) and academic achievement (Strand, Knudsen, Bower, & Swedberg, 2013). Physical education programs should serve as an effective method to educate children about the benefits of physical activity and support long term healthy lifestyle behaviors (California Department of Education, 2013).

The health benefits of physical activity are well presented. As well the important role of schools' physical education in reducing sedentary behavior and its contribution to healthy population has been identified (McKenzie & Lounsbery, 2013). Lack of physical activity and poor nutrition have been shown to influence the population at large. Regrettably, individuals with disabilities appear to be most negatively affected by the lack of physical activity. Considering that the US population includes 56 million people with disabilities (U.S. Census Bureau, 2013), 6.7 million of whom are children and youth in public schools (National Center for Education Statistics, 2014). There may be long term health and economic implications related to lack of physical activities. According to Shields, Dodd and Abblitt (2009) many children with developmental disabilities are not engaging in the recommended amount of daily physical activity. Individuals with disabilities demonstrate higher rates of sedentary behavior, lower levels of fitness, and decreased levels of overall health than nondisabled individuals (Zhang, Piwowar, & Reilly, 2009). The U.S. Government Accountability Office (2011) reported that students with disabilities participate in school-based physical education at a rate significantly and consistently lower than their nondisabled peers. Teachers attested that students with emotional and behavioral disabilities have a significant risk of uncontrolled aggression, which showed higher risk scores on children's capacity to manage their anger. This results in lack of participation in physical education (Lotan, Hadash, Amrani, Pinsker, & Weiss, 2015).

One factor associated with students' willingness to participate in physical education classes is attitude (Van Wely, Balemans, Becher, & Dallmeijer, 2014). A negative attitude towards physical education may negatively impact how students learn authentic physical skills which decreases participation in physical activities (Bernstein, Phillips, & Silverman, 2011). Teachers confirmed that students who report positive attitudes toward experiences with physical activity are likely to continue those activities into adulthood (Strean, 2011).

The relationship between learning disabilities, emotional and behavioral disabilities and attention difficulties with respect to attitudes in physical education classes have not been thoroughly explored in current literature (Collins, 2012). Teachers suggest that hyperactivity, impulsivity, disorders of memory, and disorders of attention may produce challenges for this population to abide established physical education procedures (Gaddes, 2013). Consequently, inability to follow and understand the physical education approach may generate a sedentary lifestyle for students with learning disabilities (Horowitz, 2014) which concede possibility to continue into adulthood (Craigie, Lake, Kelly, Adamson, & Mathers, 2011).

Background

Advocacy for increasing physical activity and decreasing sedentary behavior must continue at school and home by encouraging approaches to daily physical activities and decrease inactivity patterns (Abdi, 2015). Schools aggressively need to fulfill the recommended physical education curriculum. This subject should be recognized as an academic subject and part of the core curriculum content standards with conjunctions of programs such as *NFL Play60* (American Heart Association, 2015) or *Let's move* (U. S. Department of Health and Human Services, 2010).

Adaptation to a sedentary life style increases as children become older. Qualitative analysis of many related studies revealed a response relation between increased sedentary behavior and unfavorable health outcomes (Tremblay, LeBlanc, Kho, Saunders, Larouche, Colley, &Gorber, 2011). In a study with contradictory findings to prior research, of children aged five to 12, indicated that with increasing age total scores of physical fitness is improved (Fjørtoft, Pedersen, Sigmundsson, & Vereijken, 2011). Nonetheless, vast majority of evidence relies on decreasing physical activity as age increases. Beyond recommended screen-time including television, computers, phones and similar devices, physical inactivity was positively associated with age and black race/ethnicity yet negatively associated with income level (Carlson, Fulton, Lee, Foley, Heitzler, & Huhman, 2010).

A physical activity program effectively reduced adiposity and improved cardiorespiratory fitness without restrictions of dietary energy intake (Yin, Moore, Johnson, Vernon, & Gutin, 2012). The results conclude that it is critical to incorporate strategies to attract and retain the children in receiving adequate physical activity. The efforts directed at obese children determined that these children are typically less physically active than their healthy-weight peers and are often assumed to be unfit (Tsiros, Coates, Howe, Walkley, Hills, Wood, & Buckley, 2014). More than 17% of children and adolescents in the United States are obese (Office of the Surgeon General, 2010), which is a significant proportion. Healthier generations of individuals depend on physical activity's emphasis for school-age children. Unhealthy generations affect the health of nations as a result of the global epidemic of obesity due to physical inactivity.

Physical inactivity is a comprehensive international public health problem and has been linked to many of the most serious illnesses facing many industrialized nations. Nevertheless, there is little evidence examining the physical activity profile for the vulnerable population, such as people with intellectual disabilities (Lin, Lin, Lin, Chang, Wu, & Wu, 2010). The U.S. Department of Education (2016) reported that in 2013, 12.1 percent of the nation's K–12 students had disabilities.

The population of students identified as specific learning disabilities declined considerably throughout the decade, falling from 2.86 million to 2.43 million students or from 6.1 to 4.9 percent of all students nationwide (Scull & Winkler, 2011). Yet, there is a lack of research examining this population. Additional information and guidance are needed to provide and improve opportunities in physical education and sports for students with disabilities (U.S. Government Accountability Office, 2010). Research has shown that race also plays a significant role in placement of students in special education. Blacks and Hispanics are far more likely to be identified as intellectually disabled or emotionally disturbed compared to the rest of the school population (Finn, Rotherham, Hokanson, &Will, 2001).

In IDEA (Individual Disabilities Education Act) the disabilities of children aged three to 21 are identified and defined (Winnick, 2011). The collective information confirms that physical activity results in numerous health, psychological and academic benefits. Some studies have found negative but small associations between children's physical activity and academic achievement while other studies have reported positive and strong relationships between physical activity and cognitive outcomes (Fedewa & Ahn, 2011). Nevertheless in the literature the relationship has been debated (Singh, Uijtdewilligen, Twisk, Van Mechelen, & Chinapaw, 2012; Davis, Tomporowski, McDowell, Austin, Miller, Yanasak, & Naglieri, 2011; Ulstad, Halvari, Sørebø, & Deci, 2016). Therefore if the attitude of children, especially those with disabilities is changed, improving children's academic performance might transpire.

To achieve powerful action and to make schools prosper, physical educators must first understand the tremendous social shifts and technological changes (Schlechty, 2011). Physical education teachers have an obligation to teach all students. Under the strong leadership and support of the faculty for change, many transformations will take place. If the education foundation supports a range of efforts to strengthen leadership through teachers, students can improve to be engaged in a healthy lifestyle (Abdi & Juniu, 2015). Exposure to new information provokes numerous ideas; hence, well-designed programs emerge from powerful and constructive teachers' perspectives and recommendations. Consideration of teachers' perspectives can provide important information about contextual influences that can be used to bridge the research to practice gap in school-based programs (Reinke, Stormont, Herman, Puri, & Goel, 2011).

Statement of the Problem

Lack of exercise and childhood obesity have more than doubled in children and quadrupled in adolescents over the past 30 years (Ogden, Carroll, Kit, &Flegal, 2014; National Center for Health Statistics, 2015), placing children at risk for health effects such as prediabetes (et al., CDC, 2011), heart disease, asthma, diabetes, and cancer (Wang, McPherson, Marsh, Gortmaker, & Brown, 2011). Physical activity in physical education class can support healthy behavior and lifestyles (Standage, Gillison, Ntoumanis, & Treasure, 2012) but negative effects associated with a lack of exercise and increased obesity (Karnik & Kanekar, 2015). As identified by teachers, many students with learning disabilities report negative attitudes toward both physical education and physical activity (Kjonniksen, Fjortoft, & Wold, 2009). There is a strong relationship between student attitude toward physical education and participation in physical activity (Nelson, Benson, & Jensen, 2010). In fact, students who express positive attitudes toward physical activity are likely to continue those activities into adulthood.

The literature is indicating that lack of participation in physical education class is due to the perceived negative attitude of students with learning disabilities (Faison-Hodge & Porretta, 2004; et al., Collins, 2012). However, the problem is that there is limited research on how teachers perceive and assist students to participate in physical education (Eklund & Tenenbaum, 2014). Attitudes can influence whether or not a student will regularly engage in and continue to participate in physical education and activities (Subramaniam & Silverman et al., 2007). The factors associated with the perceptions that students with disabilities have a negative attitude toward physical education and resulting decrease in physical activity are not fully understood by teachers (Mercier, Phillip, & Silverman, 2016). In an effort to better understand why students are not participating in physical education, teachers' perceptions and suggested strategies for assisting children with learning disabilities was assessed. Teachers' perspectives and suggested strategies in assisting students with learning disabilities in order to increase physical activity are needed to guide physical educators to teach their students (Cheon, Reeve, & Moon, 2012; Harwell & Jackson, 2014). Recommendations suggested further research of physical activities in physical education class (Verret, Guay, Berthiaume, Gardiner, & Béliveau, 2010; Barr & Shields, 2011); with respect to teachers' perspectives and learning about their suggestions to improve physical activity in physical education class (Kohl & Cook, 2013).

Purpose of the Study

The purpose of this qualitative case study was to understand the perceptions of physical education teachers and their experiences with learning disabled students in their classes. More specifically, this research filled the gap in the literature about attitudes that learning disabled students have about physical education in school. Using teachers' perceptions, this study was designed to inform future practice related to teaching of physical education to students with learning disabilities. Teachers' perceptions of these students' attitudes toward participation in physical education was assessed through semi-structured interviews of teachers. The needs of students with disabilities are met with teachers who have positive attitudes toward inclusion (Hutchinson, Minnes, Burbidge, Dods, Pyle, & Dalton, 2015). Thus, understanding the perspectives of teachers is crucial in educational research. The population consisted of 10 teachers assigned to PreK-12 physical education classes in a district in Northeast of the United States. According to the National Center for Educational Statistics (2014) this district is a comprehensive community public school district with 9,465 students and 20 public schools, serving Pre-K to 12th grade where 1,424 students receive Individual Educational Plan. A sample of 10 teachers from 18 contacted teachers was invited to participate in this study. The district employs 38 physical education teachers and they were selected based on initial replies of first responders. Immediately after 10 teachers agreed to participate in this study the selection was terminated. Semi-structured interviews (Appendix D) contained of 10 questions guided the researcher in answering the research questions.

Research Questions

This qualitative case study was framed by two research questions which were explored through personal, one-on-one interview sessions. Two components framework of attitude, affective (enjoyment) and cognitive (usefulness) were characterized in the study. The following questions reflected vital elements of teachers' experiences and perceptions in working with learning disable students and attitude behavior of physical activity during physical education class. The outcome of this research will contribute to assist teachers with the attitudes of learning disabled students in physical education class. The applications emerging from the study will be those best practices that are suggested by the interviews.

- Q 1. What are physical education teachers' perceptions and experiences in working with learning disabled students in their classes with respect to enjoyment and usefulness attitude components?
- Q 2. How would physical education teachers describe the attitudes and behaviors of learning disabled students in their classrooms?

Nature of the Study

In the proposed research, qualitative method was used to gather data. This method was employed in order to understand the factors associated with the physical education teachers' perceptions and experiences in educating students with learning disabilities respecting enjoyment and usefulness attitude components. In addition to understanding how physical education teachers describe the attitudes and behaviors of learning disabled students in their classrooms. Utilizing teachers' perceptions and their suggested strategies, this study was designed to assist and inform future practice related to teaching of physical education to students with learning disabilities. Teachers' perceptions of these students' attitudes and participation in physical education was assessed through semi-structured interviews of teachers.

The intent of qualitative research is to understand and explore the complexities of a particular social setting, situation, event, group or interaction (Creswell, 2012). As a result, a qualitative method was chosen to provide tools for the researcher with investigation of the phenomenon within its real-life in an educational setting context. This study was researched qualitatively based on several factors; a) the research addressed "what" and "how" questions, b) information was collected without changing the environment, and c) information obtained was about the naturally occurring setting. This method was the most suitable for the study.

According to Thomas (2011), case studies are analyses of persons, events, decisions, periods, projects, policies, institutions, or other systems that are studied holistically by one or more methods. Therefore case study was used to describe the phenomenon and the real-life context (Yin, 2011). The settings of this case study was a district in the Northeastern United States with a high percentage of African American students, low achievement scores on state mandated tests, and a high percentage of students on free or reduced lunch (US News and World Report, 2013).

The proposed sample included 10 physical education teachers from K to twelfth grade in a district with 1,424 students with learning disabilities. All physical education teachers teach students with learning disabilities at self-contained, inclusion or both settings. The Department of Special Education Services provides resources to students with disabilities within this district. The department furnishes assistance for eligible students ages 3-21 years old in Self-Contained Learning Disabilities, Self-Contained Autism, Self-Contained Multiple Disabilities, Self-Contained Behavioral Disabilities, Self-Contained Cognitive Impaired (mild/moderate), Self-Contained Preschool Disabilities, and Inclusion when needed. According to Tashakkori and Teddlie, (2010) the purposive sampling involves selecting participants based on a specific purpose; therefore, the small number of participants provides more in-depth information about a particular phenomenon.

In a study at the University of Wisconsin (2014), it is indicated, "Data Collection is an important aspect of any type of research study. Inaccurate data collection can impact the results of a study and ultimately lead to invalid results" (para1). For the purposes of this study qualitative data was collected through teacher interviews. Two research questions were explored through personal, one-on-one interview sessions with 10 teachers. During personal interviews of 10 proposed physical education teachers, participants were expected to share their personal views, beliefs, and experiences that would present further understanding of students with learning disabilities' attitudes and how to assist such students to increase their physical activity. Interviews were utilized as the design for data collection, to give participants an opportunity to provide their own explanations and reflections (Roulston, 2010). Following the interview sessions, all digital recorded data were transcribed precisely into Microsoft Word at a personal computer.

Significance of the Study

The number of children with disabilities served under IDEA as of December 1, 2011, in the state of New Jersey was 107,010 students which covers 16.5% of all students while the national average was at 12.9% (Data display: New Jersey, 2011). In a study Kriemler, Meyer, Martin, Van Sluijs, Andersen, and Martin, (2011), confirmed the potential of high quality public health and school-based physical activity interventions for increasing physical activity and possibly fitness in youth. Nonetheless, in previous studies, it has been shown that even general education teachers with positive attitudes towards inclusion are unenthusiastic in receiving students with disabilities in their classrooms (Hwang & Evans, 2011). The behavioral beliefs of teachers vary according to the disability conditions of the students; however, there is no significant effect of demographic factors on the beliefs of physical education teachers teaching students with disabilities (Wang, Qi, & Wang, 2015). Uniform research dated back more than 10 years, confirms that people with disabilities are far less likely to engage in physically active lifestyles (Rimmer, Riley, Wang, Rauworth, & Jurkowski, 2004).

Based on what is known, the significance of this study was to understand the attitudes of learning disabled students concerning enjoyment and usefulness. With respect to understanding if students were not participating in physical education class due to their negative attitude, as research suggests. The research took into account teachers' perceptions and suggested strategies for assisting children with learning disabilities. From theory to practice, such findings would influence the decisions of local school officials, teachers, and state policy makers regarding physical education programs in the school setting. This research may eventually support a significant portion of the population in physical activity at physical education classes which have not taken into account.

Definition of Key Terms

Attitude. In earlier work in the history, when attention started given to attitude, Allport (1934) described attitude as a two component construct consisting of 1) an emotional attraction or feeling (affective) toward 2) responses to objects, situations, and beliefs (cognitive) about the characteristics of an attitude object study (Subramaniam & Silverman, 2007).

Curriculum. In formal education, a curriculum is the set of courses and contents offered at a school or university (Fink, 2013). Moreover, Beyer and Davis (2012) explained designing instruction for students is shaped by teachers' ability to apply a variety of personal resources including their pedagogical content knowledge. According to development patterns, curriculum resources can be divided into 1) existing curriculum resources, 2) potential curriculum resources and 3) void curriculum resources (Li & Sun, 2013).

Disability. Disability is an umbrella term covering impairments, activity limitations, and participation restrictions (Shakespeare, 2013). Other sources define disability as an impairment in body function or structure, in addition to an activity limitation which cause difficulty encountered by an individual in executing a task or action. While a participation restriction is a problem experienced by an individual who is involvement in life situations (World Health Organization [WHO], 2016).

Elementary School. At elementary school, primary education is delivered for students between the ages of 5 to 12 years old who are in between Pre-Kindergarten and secondary education. (U.S. Department of Education, 2016).

Exercise. Exercise is considered any bodily activity that improves or maintains physical fitness, wellness and health (Wang, Li, Dong, Zhang, & Zhang, 2015). The Office of Disease Prevention and Health Promotion (2016) described exercise as a subcategory of physical activity that is planned, structured, repetitive, and purposive in the sense that the improvement or maintenance of one or more components of physical fitness is the objective.

Health education. Educating people about different areas of health is called health education. It was described as the profession of educating people about health (Sharma, 2016) which is aligned with the World Health Organization belief on (2016) that health education is any combination of learning experiences designed to help individuals and communities improve their health by increasing their knowledge or influencing their attitudes.

Inclusion. In the 'full inclusion' setting, the students with special needs are always educated alongside with students without special needs, as the first and desired option while maintaining appropriate supports and services (Crockett & Kauffman, 2013). Children are more likely to have their learning needs met in a non-segregated setting of education that embodies principles of Differentiated Instruction to establish various levels of inclusion (Conway, 2014).

Individualized Education Program. An Individual Education Program (IEP) is defined as the individualized objectives of a child who has been found with a disability, as defined by federal regulations (Allen, 2015). The IEP is intend to help children reach educational goals more easily than they otherwise would succeed. In a document by the New York City Department of Education (2014), IEP refers to the special education and related services specifically designed to meet the unique educational needs of a student with a disability.

Obesity. Obesity is the easiest medical condition to recognize but one of the hardest to treat. Centers for Disease Control and Prevention, (2015) defined obesity as a Body Mass Index (BMI) at or above the 95th percentile for children of the same age and gender. BMI is calculated using height and weight (Flegal, Carroll, Kit, & Ogden, 2012).

Other Health Impairment. Other Health Impairment (OHI) is one of the 14 categories of disability listed on the national special education law is the Individuals with Disabilities Education Act (IDEA). National Dissemination Center for Children with Disabilities, (2012) determined that under IDEA, a child who has 'other health impairment' is likely to be eligible for special services including educational, developmental, and functional needs resulting from a disability.

Physical activity. According to Centers for Disease Control and Prevention (2008), physical activity refers to any bodily movement produced by the contraction and extension of skeletal muscle which increases energy expenditure above a basal level that enhances health.

Physical education. Physical education is a subject taken during primary and secondary grades to promote play or movement exploration to advance a healthy lifestyle (Kirk, 2014). The National Association for Sport and Physical Education (2014) describes the goal of physical education to develop physically literate individuals who have the knowledge, skills, and confidence to enjoy a lifetime of healthful physical activity.

Professional development. According to Speck and Knipe (2005), professional development includes all types of facilitated learning opportunities, ranging from college degrees to formal coursework, conferences and informal learning opportunities situated in practice. It has been described as intensive and collaborative, ideally incorporating an evaluative stage.

Psychomotor learning. Psychomotor learning refers to the relationship between cognitive functions and physical movement. Researchers at Emporia State University (2016) confirmed that psychomotor is a domain which deals with manual or physical skills.

Quality Assurance. Quality assurance and quality in education refer to the excellent work of a teacher that also has a significant effect on students (Biggs, 2011).

Specific Learning Disability. Based on American Speech-Language-Hearing Association (2014), Specific Learning Disability (SLD) is explained as a disorder in one or more of the basic psychological processes. This processed is involved in understanding or in using language, spoken or written, in which the disorder may manifest itself in the imperfect ability to listen, think, speak, read, write, spell, or do mathematical calculations.

Student with a disability. Individuals with Disabilities Education Act explained that a student with a disability is a student with a documented Specific Learning Disability (SLD), Emotional Behavioral Disability (EBD), or Other Health Impairment (OHI) due to attention difficulties listed under OHI. As a result such student receives special education and related services as outlined in an IEP (Murdick, Gartin, & Fowler, 2013).

Teacher education. Teacher education refers to the policies and measures designed to equip prospective teachers with the knowledge, attitudes, behaviors, and skills that are required to perform the tasks effectively in the classroom, school, and wider community (Vaidya, 2014). In a seminal work Raza, Afridi, and Ali (2013) indicated that there is a longstanding and ongoing debate about the most appropriate term to describe the activities.

Summary

This proposed qualitative case study was conducted to address the teachers' perspective of children with learning disabilities in respect to enjoyment and usefulness. Students with learning disabilities are at higher risk for decreased participation in physical education class due to their attitude (Collins et al., 2012). The factors associated with students' attitude toward physical education are not fully understood (Mercier, Phillips, & Silverman et al., 2016). Therefore teachers' perspectives are important to describe the attitudes and behaviors of learning disabled students. Teachers' perspective provide districts with knowledgeable data on how students respond to learning in an active environment (Smith, 2012).

Interview techniques were used to gather data directly from samples of physical education teachers to answer two research questions. The research questions contributed to purpose of the study, which is to understand the perceptions of physical education teachers and their experiences with learning disabled students in their classes. More specifically, this research filled the gap in the literature about attitudes that learning disabled students have about physical education in school. The purpose was not only to understand the teachers' perspective but to realize how to improve students' physical activity in physical education with learning disabilities, using teachers' perceptions. This study was designed to inform future practice related to teaching of physical education to students with learning disabilities.

The research from this study would add to the quality of literature related to teachers' perspectives on attitudes of students with learning disabilities toward physical education. This information would assist educators, principals, superintendants, and policy makers to construct decisions on the learning disability population within the physical education setting. Additionally, the results can be used by educators to examine alternative ways to teach and maximize the participation levels of their students in physical education with learning disabilities.

Chapter 2

Literature Review

Strong scientific evidence indicates that physical activity is positively associated with health and educational performance of students (Bouchard, Blair, & Haskell, 2012; Edwards, Mauch, & Winkelman, 2011). However, physical inactivity is the fourth leading cause of death worldwide (Kohl, Craig, Lambert, Inoue, Alkandari, Leetongin, & Lancet, 2012). Despite known benefits of regular physical activity for health and well-being, many researchers report levels of physical activity in young people are low and decline dramatically during adolescence (Belton, O'Brien, Meegan, Woods, & Issartel, 2014). A critical review of the literature revealed moderate to strong evidence that physical activity positively affects balance, muscle strength, and quality of life in individuals with intellectual disabilities (Bartlo & Klein, 2011); however, lack of physical activity for children with disabilities is evident (Phillips & Holland 2011; Spencer-Cavaliere & Watkinson, 2010).

The purpose of this qualitative case study was to understand the perceptions of physical education teachers and their experiences with learning disabled students in their classes. More specifically, this research filled the gap in the literature about attitudes that learning disabled students have about physical education in school. Lack of exercise is a serious public health concern for the general population. However, it is of greater concern for individuals with disabilities as they are at much greater risk of physical inactivity (Wen, Wai, Tsai, Yang, Cheng, Lee, & Wu, 2011). Using teachers' perceptions and suggestive strategies, this study was designed to aid and inform future practices related to teaching of physical education to students with learning disabilities.

For the purposes of this study, a thorough review was presented of the literature focused on students with learning disabilities and their attitudes. Evident in this review was the underrepresentation of students with disabilities in the research.

Not only there is more research related to attitudes of students without disabilities towards students with disabilities; (Townsend, 2008) there is a lack of research on the attitudes of students with disabilities towards physical education (Nowicki & Sandieson, 2002).

Research on students with disabilities is not well represented in the literature (Collins et al., 2012). In an investigation, James, Kellman, and Lieberman (2011) revealed most researchers who examined the attitudes of students with disabilities in physical education programs, at any level in school, largely assessed the topic from the perspective of the general physical education teachers or nondisabled students. There is a general absence of research specifically examining the perceptions of students with disabilities.

Physical education teachers are expected to educate all students, including those with disabilities; however this can be challenging, particularly when a future or current teacher does not appreciate or understand the challenges of working with a disability. Using a collaborative approach between adapted physical education teachers and general physical education teachers may be the most effective in increasing general physical education teacher efficacy when working with children with disabilities (Umhoefer, Vargas, & Beyer, 2015). Of note, the use of adapted physical education service approaches has positive efficacy on general physical education when working with students with disabilities.

This literature review started with attitude theory and next advanced to expansion of students' attitude in physical education and areas of influence. The relationship between disabilities and healthy lifestyle, and physical education as an academic subject were exposed subsequently. The review continued with hidden disabilities and concluded with teachers' perspective after all grounds were covered.

Documentation

The literature review for this research study was conducted by examining, searching, and investigating scholarly educational peer-reviewed journals, relevant non-educational peer-reviewed journals, relevant textbooks, organizational websites in addition to sources from states and federal government sponsored websites or professional organizations. Education Resources Information Center (ERIC), ProQuest databases, Roadrunner, EBSCOhost, SAGE Journals provided by the Northcentral University (NCU) library were used in addition to online searches for applicable materials, such as Education Research Complete and Teachers College Record. A combination of keywords and phrases were utilized to search the related information. To demonstrate the confirmation of historical aspects of the study, older research is included in the literature review; yet, the majority of the resources were limited to publications within the past five years.

Attitude Theory

Attitude is difficult to define as it is a complex concept that is changeable, measurable and influences the person's emotions and behavior and can be formed from a person's past and present (Allport, 1935). Moving from this early notion, Eagly and Chaiken (1998) defined attitude as a psychological tendency expressed by evaluating a particular entity with some degree of favor or disfavor. Ajzen (2001) suggested it is common to define an attitude as affect toward an object (i.e., discrete emotions or overall arousal) and is generally understood to be distinct from attitude as a measure of favorability. Similarly, Crano and Prislin (2006) stated attitudes represent an evaluative integration of cognitions and affects experienced in relation to an object.

Subramaniam and Silverman (2007) suggested that attitude can influence whether or not a student will regularly engage in and continue to participate in physical education and activities. As students with disabilities engage in significantly less physical activity than their nondisabled peers, attitudes are particularly important for this population. Attitudes of children with disabilities change based on the attached stigma which has received much attention in psychiatric disability research (Werner, Corrigan, Ditchman, & Sokol, 2012). However, further development of measures to assess public, self, and family stigma related to intellectual disability is desirable.

Expansion of Attitude: Affective and Cognitive Components

Attitude in physical education suggests two components of learning; affective and cognitive. An early notion described attitude as a construct comprised of both cognitive and affective elements (Bagozzi & Burnkrant, 1985). Later attempts to define attitude included a three component model of (a) affect, (b) cognition, and (c) behavior (Subramaniam & Silverman, 2000) suggesting that feelings and beliefs affect behavior toward an attitudinal object. Dismore and Bailey (2010) suggested that the components include two factors: (1) an affective component measuring degree of emotional attraction or feeling, and (2) a cognitive component accounting for beliefs.

There has been a longstanding interest in affective characteristics of both educational and corporate environments and each domain has produced its own set of theorists and research (Gable & Wolf, 2012). Learning is connected to the affective domain and physical education focuses on feelings, values, social behavior, and attitudes related to human movement (Holt, Brett, Hannon, & James, 2006). Researchers mentioned that learning in the affective domain often translates to learning concepts such as sportsmanship, fair play, respect for others, and respect for equipment, self-control, responsibility, and motivation. A more recent study implies that physical educators have a responsibility to intentionally incorporate appropriate affective qualities and attitudes as part of their teaching objectives and learning outcomes (Heidorn & Welch, 2010). The study draws attention to two of the National Standards for Physical Education that specifically addresses both personal and social behavior. These two standards are related to respect of self and others in physical activity settings and valuing the physical activity for health, enjoyment, challenge, self-expression, and/or social interaction (NASPE, 2014).

According to Kirk, Gray, Riby, and Cornish, (2015), attention and working memory have been strongly associated with academic achievement, language development, and behavioral stability. The authors suggested that children who are susceptible to cognitive and learning problems caused by an underlying intellectual disability, execute difficulties.

Following a study designed to analyze the effects of an intervention on cognitive performance in physical education, Ardoy, Fernández-Rodríguez, Jiménez-Pavón, Castillo, Ruiz, and Ortega (2014) suggested that the intensity of physical education sessions might produce a role in the positive effect of physical activity on cognition and academic success. The study was conducted in 67 adolescents and cognitive performance including: non-verbal and verbal ability, abstract reasoning, spatial ability, verbal reasoning and numerical ability was assessed. Furthermore, academic achievement was measured by school grades. The researchers concluded that increased physical education can benefit cognitive performance and academic achievement. In the cognitive domain, students learn information of how to keep physically fit and live long and healthy lives.

Students' Attitudes in Physical Education: Areas of Influence

Several influential areas toward students' attitudes in physical education exist within the literature. In this section the contemporary research on students' attitudes toward physical education is reviewed. For the better understanding of how teachers can help students with disabilities to achieve higher amounts of physical activity in physical education class, one must have an understanding of the influential factors. These factors associate with perception understanding that students with disabilities have a negative attitude toward physical education, which result in decreased physical activity. The variables of (a) gender and (b) grade level and age which are the most significant will be discussed in this section.

Gender. The debate about co-education versus single-sex groups in physical education has been studied from a socio-cultural perspective in physical education (Sykes, 2011). Proponents of single-sex education suggest that separation of boys and girls, by classrooms or schools, increases students' achievement and academic interest (Pahlke, Hyde, & Allison, 2014). In another study, Arabaci (2009) revealed that attitudes were more positive for boys than girls in separation. However results from different studies do not support this view. It is noted in a research study conducted by Bibik, Goodwin, and Orsega-Smith (2007) that the majority of general and disabled students preferred coeducational learning experiences.

Scholz, Gebhardt, and Tobias (2012) focused on attitudes of teachers and student teachers in the field of special education towards integration of children with disabilities in regular schools. Results of their study suggested that there is support for the idea of coeducation. Almost 60% of teachers in the field of special education think integration has a positive impact on school development. Seventy-eight percent of teachers and 96.3 percent of students majoring in intellectual disabilities share the opinion that the coeducation of children would work well.

Findings also suggested that there are significant gender differences in physical activity. In addition to natural active lifestyle, boys tend to spend more time engaging in physical activity (Kamtsios, 2010). Evidence offered that from an early age, differences in gender-based attitudes towards opportunities for sports and physical activities have a significant influence on children's participation (Bailey, Wellard, & Dismore, 2014). Kamtsios (2012) studied775 children (362 boys and 413 girls) attending their fifth and sixth year of elementary school and concluded that physical education programs should encourage both boys' and girls' participation due to the influence of long term exercises behaviors. The recommendation was that physical educators should pay attention to gender differences to provide involvement, enjoyment, and success for both boys and girls.

Consistent with previous research found in the literature, results revealed that instructions that induce as external focus of attentions can enhance motor learning in children with learning disabilities (Chiviacowsky, Wulf, & Avila, 2013). This study examined whether the learning benefits of attention's external focus on the movement effect is relative to an internal focus found previously in non-disabled children and adults would also be found in children with intellectual disabilities. During the study the gender difference in throwing performance was recorded which showed that boys typically have a longer stride in throwing.

Grade level and age. Positive attitude toward physical education exhibits a decline as age and grade level incline. In a nationally representative survey of students' attitudes toward physical education, 77% of children aged nine to13 years old reported participation in free-time physical activity during the previous seven days (Center for Disease Control and Prevention, 2010). However three years after this finding, the Center for Disease Control and Prevention (2013) reported that participation in physical activity declines as young people age.

Relatedly, statistically significant decrease of physical activity in high school was reported. Only 29% percent of high school students had participated, in physical activity, at least 60 minutes per day on each of the seven days before the survey. In the same study, 14% of high school students had not participated in 60 or more minutes of physical activity on any day during the seven days before the survey. Additionally, Hünük & Demirhan, (2010) suggested middle school boys and girls in grades six through eight have declined in physical education due to developmental differences of grade levels and possible repetition in the curriculum.

Physical Education as an Academic Subject and Its Influence on Academics

Historic context. There are two historically relevant perspectives related to physical education. In one perspective, the mind and body were thought to stand together in the closest correlation to provide academic recognition of physical education (Schaeffer, 1891). Alternatively, Davidson (1896) explained that in Greek educational discipline, education was divided into mental education and physical education consistent with original aim of goodness including bravery of soul and strength of body. As time passed, these aims underwent considerable changes and physical education became more focused on beauty and grace, while mental education extended its efforts to the power of the minds and divided itself into literary and music education.

Physical education is known for its impact on academic achievement in the medical field since 1964. In fact, many directors of physical education of the preceding generation were medical doctors (Henry, 1964). Prior to that, considerable time elapsed before the teachers of physical education had academic standing

(Elliott, 1930). The United States Department of Education does not define physical education as an academic subject. However, under *de facto* definition by various requirements for a content area, physical education has all the characteristics in place for an academic subject (National Association for Sports and Physical Education, 2016). Thus, there is an adequate relationship to accept physical education as an academic subject

The influence of physical education on academics and cognitive learning was exposed in the early 1900s. In an early study, Johnson (1942) argued that there is no significant relationship between physical skill and academic grades but a hint of a relationship exists between skills and grades in physical education class. Recent evidence suggests regular physical activity can positively influence academic performance which will be explored further in this chapter.

Relationship between physical activity and academics. Results from studies by the U.S. Department of Health and Human Services (2010) on the relationship between academics and physical activity are somewhat inconclusive. For example, one study suggested that physical activity is either positively related to academic performance (50.5% of the associations summarized) or that there is not a demonstrated relationship between physical activity and academic performance (48% of the associations summarized). Furthermore, increasing time during the school day to dedicate to physical activity does not appear to deduct from academic performance.

There is increasing evidence for the association between physical activity and cognitive function. Furthermore, the evidence suggested that these variables are linked to academic achievement. Many studies have confirmed the positive relationship between physical education and improving academics (Donnelly & Lambourne, 2011; Rasberry, Lee, Robin, Laris, Russell, Coyle, & Nihiser, 2011; Correa-Burrows, Burrows, Ibaceta, Orellana, & Ivanovic, 2014).

A handful of schools are reducing or eliminating physical education classes in efforts to increase time available for other subjects. This may not be the best approach, as research findings support the idea that dedicating and developing time during the school day for physical education class does not compromise academic performance of other subjects (Carlson, Fulton, Lee, Maynard, Brown, Kohl and Dietz, 2008). The finding is supported by Chomitz, Slining, McGowan, Mitchell, Dawson and Hacker (2009), who reported a positive relationship between physical education and performance on standardized tests.

In a contrary study, Nunlist (2013) suggested that physical activity, including school physical education programs, have no effect on academic performance. Rather, certain types of coordinated activity may improve student's concentration and attention. In examining the association between physical activity and academic performance in a relatively large sample of children and adolescents, Esteban-Cornejo, Tejero-González, Martinez-Gomez, Cabanas-Sánchez, Fernández-Santos, Conde-Caveda, and Veiga (2014), added a semi-similar view to the debate. Their three-year longitudinal study analyzed 1,778 children and adolescents ages six-18 years old.

The authors concluded that physical activity may influence academic performance during both childhood and adolescence. However, the association was negative and very weak. The results indicated that physical activity was contrary associated with all academic performance. Additionally, the researchers recommended more longitudinal and intervention studies.

Cardiorespiratory fitness and academics. Cardiorespiratory fitness is a large part of physical education programs and has been associated with cognition. Neveetheless, the magnitude of this association remains unknown (Haapala, 2013). Various elements of physical fitness in children have shown a declining trend during the past few decades (Abdi et al, 2015). Generally, research on academics and cardiorespiratory fitness is focused on the relationship between motor skills and cognitive functioning. Moore, Drollette, Scudder, Bharij, and Hillman (2014) assessed the influence of cardiorespiratory fitness on arithmetic cognition measured by a standardized mathematics achievement test of 40, nine-10 year old children. The study concluded that the benefits of cardiorespiratory fitness extend to arithmetic cognition, which has important implications for the educational environment and the context of learning.

The results of a cross-sectional review (Haapala et al., 2013) concluded that high levels of cardiorespiratory fitness and motor skills may be beneficial for cognitive development and academic performance; but, the evidence relies mainly on cross-sectional studies. The authors suggested that children with higher cardiorespiratory fitness have more efficient cognitive processing in comparison to children with lower cardiorespiratory fitness.

The global epidemic of inactivity not only produces obesity rather has detrimental implications for young people's cognitive function and academic achievement (Kantomaa, Stamatakis, Kankaanpää, Kaakinen, Rodriguez, Taanila, & Tammelin, 2013). The above study was designed to assess two relationships 1) relationship between physical activity and a higher grade-point average and 2) relationship between obesity's connections with a lower grade-point average both in adolescences. Moreover, researchers specified that motor functions in childhood had a negative indirect effect on adolescents' academic achievement via physical inactivity and obesity but not through cardiorespiratory fitness. Thus, physical activity and obesity may be related to childhood motor function and adolescents' academic achievement. Additionally, an important factor motivating the effects of obesity and physical inactivity on academic underachievement might be the cooperation of motor function in childhood.

Physical activity impact on academic performance of children with a disability. Not many studies have been published on physical activity's impact of students with intellectual disabilities in relation to academic performance which will be discussed in this section. Nonetheless, this section starts with examining the children with learning disabilities and their academic impact on students without disabilities to establish a case of equal opportunities. The lack of fitness and recreation opportunities for children with disabilities are problematic and can be consequential to proper health and development (Clapham & Lamont, 2015). The section further moves to students with learning disabilities and lack of equal options.

Sermier, Dessemontet, and Bless (2013) conducted a study to measure the influence of integrating children with an intellectual disability into general education classrooms. The students with disabilities were placed in classrooms and provided support with their low, average, and high-achieving peers without disability. The experiment was conducted with an experimental group of 202 pupils from classrooms with an included child with mild or moderate intellectual disability and a control group of 202 pupils from classrooms with no included children with special educational needs. The progress of these two groups was compared over a period of one school year for academic achievement. The results revealed no significant difference in the progress of the low, average, or high-achieving pupils from classrooms with or without inclusion. In conclusion the research suggested that children with an intellectual disability in primary grades with supported general education classrooms do not have a negative impact on the progress of pupils without a disability.

Research have already established the impact of physical activity on brain and cognitive function. In a 16-day period, Everhart, Dimon, Stone, Desmond, and Casilio (2012) asked students to participate in a series off aerobic exercises guided by a commercial DVD and supervised by a classroom teacher. The participants were seven primary grade students and six intermediate elementary grade students with intellectual disabilities who were engaged in daily structured physical activity lesson. The physical education was offered twice within a six-day cycle. The intermediate students consistently improved academic work following the physical activity while inconsistent performance was seen in more of the primary aged students. Teachers of both classrooms commented that their students appeared to be focused more on classwork following the physical activity sessions.

In an attempt to discover how the decline in physical activity may affect academic achievement, Howie and Pate (2012) conducted a meta-analysis on the effects of physical education on cognition and academic achievement in children for more than 50 years. A total of 125 published articles were examined and authors reported the overall quality of the studies has increased but results continue to be inconsistent. The majority of conclusions of studied articles show a positive effect of physical activity as related to academic achievement. Nonetheless, the focus on academic achievement has increased as physical activity opportunities in schools have decreased. Furthermore, it was suggested that studies should use strong research designs to examine the types of physical activity needed to produce improvements in academic achievement.

In a recent study of 74 preadolescent children, no significant associations were found between Moderate-to-Vigorous Physical Activity (MVPA) in inhibition, working memory, or academic achievement (Pindus, Drollette, Scudder, Khan, Raine, Sherar, & Hillman, 2016). Aerobic fitness was positively associated with inhibitory control and spelling but not associated with other cognitive or academic variables.

In a quantitative analysis of 10,394 children in Minnesota with maltreatment histories, 32% of children were eligible for special education services and 73% had mild cognitive or behavioral disabilities (Haight, Kayama, Kincaid, Evans, & Kim, 2013). Researchers indicated that specific learning disabilities counted as frequent primary disability category was 33% and emotional/behavioral disabilities were at 27%. Children with maltreatment histories and mild cognitive or behavioral disabilities scored significantly lower than children with maltreatment histories and no identified disabilities on standardized assessments of math and reading.

Interventions for Preventing Childhood Obesity

The term obesity started appearing regularly in the literature in late 1900s. A review of epidemiologic literature published between 1970 and 1992 found consistent positive association between obesity in childhood and obesity in adulthood, (Serdula, Ivery, Coates, Freedman, Williamson, & Byers, 1993). Obese children are at increased risk of becoming obese adults (Ogden's et al., 2014) and no national success stories have been reported in the past 33 years (Ng, Fleming, Robinson, Thomson, Graetz, Margono, & Abraham, 2014). Regardless, children who are overweight are likely to become adults who are obese (Biro & Wien, 2010) therefore, urgent global action and leadership are needed to help countries in more effectively intervenes.

Between 1980 and 2000 the dramatic increases in childhood and adolescent obesity may have plateaued (Singh, Kogan, & van Dyck, 2010). But, then since 2003-2004 in particular, obesity among American young people, aged two to 19 years, has not changed significantly and remains at about 17 percent. Nevertheless, among two-five years old, obesity has declined based on the Center for Disease Control's (CDC) and National Health and Nutrition Examination Survey's (NHANES) data (Ogden, et al., 2014). To confirm this statement, high quality evidence has emerged from nine countries including the United States which suggested that the rise in the prevalence of childhood obesity has slowed appreciably, or even leveled (Olds, Maher, Zumin, Péneau, Lioret, Castetbon, & Summerbell, 2011).

Data from 1999 and 2010 indicates that obesity prevalence differs among racial and ethnic groups and also varies by age, sex, and adult head of household's income and education level (May, Freedman, Sherry & Blanck, 2013). Obesity and associated chronic conditions are endemic among the American population with rates disproportionately high among ethnic minorities and the economically disadvantaged (O'Dare, 2011).

The body of research is intense with extensive reviews assessing the effect of obesity prevention interventions for children (Summerbell, Waters, Edmunds, Kelly, Brown & Campbell, 2005; Flodmark, Marcus, & Britton 2006; Kamath, Vickers, Ehrlich, McGovern, Johnson, Singhal, & Montori, 2008; Waters, de Silva-Sanigorski, Hall, Brown, Campbell, Gao & Summerbell, 2011). The prevalence of obesity among high-socioeconomic status adolescents has decreased in recent years, whereas the prevalence of obesity among their low-socioeconomic status peers has continued to increase (Frederick, Snellman, & Putnam, 2014).

An investigation using a sample of 45,897 youth in the United States from 10 to 17 years of age showed the likelihood that youth with learning disabilities and attention-deficit/hyperactivity disorder are obese, physically inactive, and have sedentary lifestyle. Results indicated that youth with comorbid learning disabilities and attention-deficit/hyperactivity were significantly more likely than their peers without a learning disability or attention-deficit/hyperactivity to be obese (Cook & Heinrich, 2015).

In an examination of the obesity prevalence, individuals with intellectual disability had a high risk of developing obesity and women with intellectual disability had a high risk of developing morbid obesity (Hsieh, Rimmer, & Heller, 2014). On the contrary, little evidence was found to support the view that childhood obesity is an independent risk factor for adult blood lipid status, insulin levels, metabolic syndrome or type 2 diabetes (Lloyd, Langley-Evans, & McMullen, 2012).

The role of obesity. In a study Diament (2011) reported that over 36 percent of kids, ages 10 to 17 with special needs are overweight or obese compared to about 30 percent of other children. A report completed by Children with Special Healthcare Needs (2007), suggested roughly 14 to 19 percent of U.S. children have one or more of these conditions: chronic physical, developmental, behavioral, or emotional condition. The lack of empirical investigation including students with disabilities as a population of study suggested a need for further research in this area (James, Keller, & Lieberman, et al., 2011).

The key factor that affects the success of shaping positive attitudes towards regular life-long performance of physical activity is the students' level of inner motivation (Kurková, Nemček, & Labudová, 2015). Having a higher percentage of positive views are important in inner motivation of pupils' efforts towards physical education. Evidence indicates that children with disabilities have a higher rate of obesity than children without disabilities. Therefore, infusing positive inner motivation in physical activity is imperative.

Additionally, many children with disabilities also face serious health-related conditions and are affected by the current obesity crisis. Disappointingly, little is known of the actual magnitude of the problem in this population (Bandini, Danielson, Esposito, Foley, Fox, Frey, & Rodgers, 2015). Youth with intellectual and developmental disabilities are more vulnerable than the typical population to become overweight and often experience overweight and obesity at higher rates than their typically developing peers (Grondhuis & Aman, 2014). The higher risk of obesity in children with a disability resulting from less physical activity and poorer quality dietary habits than their non-disabled peers, provides some insights for researchers as to the specific components that should be considered when planning interventions (McPherson, Keith, & Swift, 2014).

In children and youth with a disability, the risk of obesity is higher and is associated with lower levels of physical activity, inappropriate eating behaviors, and chronic health conditions (Hinckson, Dickinson, Water, Sands, & Penman, 2013). Therefore, prevention should concentrate on these interventions. However, if a physical education teacher is unable to consider the facts due to unpreparedness, then the task becomes challenging.

Few studies have compared overweight or obese in intellectually disabled and non-intellectually disabled children. In a study of 218 children with intellectual disabilities and 229 children with nonintellectual disabilities Slevin, Truesdale-Kennedy, McConkey, Livingstone, and Fleming (2014), compared the prevalence of overweight or obese due to physical activity, and dietary behavior in two groups of children. The children completed a food intake and physical activity questionnaire and had body mass index and waist circumference measurements. The results indicated that significantly more students with intellectual disabilities were overweight or obese based on body mass index. Students with intellectual disabilities not only had significantly higher waist circumferences but also consumed more fatty and sugary food. This group spent most of their time engaging in low levels of activity such as reading, watching TV, and listening to music.

Obesity, overweight, and underweight among US adolescents with and without autism and other learning and behavioral developmental disabilities with health consequences of obesity were assessed (Phillips, Schieve, Visser, Boulet, Sharma, Kogan, & Yeargin-Allsopp, 2014). The researchers concluded that obesity is high among adolescents with autism and other developmental disabilities. Obesity, as well poses added chronic health risks such as common respiratory, gastrointestinal, dermatological and neurological conditions and symptoms. Similarly, Doody and Doody (2012) demonstrated that for people with intellectual disability, obesity is a significant health problem which leads to a higher risk of developing chronic conditions, such as diabetes and heart disease. In the same study, it was suggested that obesity prevention and management approaches for this population need further consideration as healthcare services have predominantly focused on the primary disability rather than on prevention.

The influence of parental factors on obesity in children with disabilities remains unclear. The current literature on obesity in typically developing children shows that the family context, and specifically the way parents treat their children are major determinants of childhood obesity (McGillivray, McVilly, Skouteris, & Boganin, 2013). Research suggests that obesity in children and adolescents with disabilities may be associated with socioeconomic status in addition to parents' own body mass index, perception and attitude towards their children's weight and physical activity, and levels of activity in both parents and children (Brunet, Sabiston, O'Loughlin, Mathieu, Tremblay, Barnett, & Lambert, 2014; Besharat Pour, Bergström, Bottai, Kull, Wickman, Håkansson, & Moradi, 2014).

Little is known about the effect of physical education on children's weight. However, results of several studies indicated that physical education lowers body mass index and reduces the probability of obesity (Cawley, Frisvold, & Meyerhoefer, 2013; Fradkin, Wallander, Elliott, Cuccaro, & Schuster, 2014; Robbins, Mallya, Polansky, & Schwarz, 2015). Nevertheless, each study had its individual results. Cawley et al. (2013), provided some evidence of physical education's effect on youth obesity thus, offering some support for the assumptions behind the Center for Disease Control recommendations to increase the amount of time that elementary school children spend in physical education classes.

Findings from the study of Fradkin el al. (2014), suggested that the reduced rate of obesity generally attributed to physical activity may not be consistent across racial/ethnic and gender groups of early adolescents. Fradkin el al. (2014) examined whether daily or almost daily lower-intensity physical activity was associated with reduced obesity in 4824 African American, Hispanic, and White youth. Participants were assessed in fifth and seventh grades. Regular lower-intensity physical activity was associated with reduced obesity only among Hispanic and White males and only in seventh grade. Fifth graders did not show reduced obesity. Additionally, neither females nor African American males or females experienced decreased obesity.

In a study in Philadelphia, Robbins et al. (2015), reported that the Comprehensive School Wellness Policy with provisions on competitive food, physical activity and nutrition education in 2006 has had little to no impact. Prevalence of unhealthy weight remains unacceptably high among public school children. Public health continues to identify effective means of preventing obesity in children and helping those affected with a healthier weight.

The Relationship Between Disabled Children, Healthy Lifestyle and Physical Education

Few international studies of children and adolescents have included comprehensive indicators of lifestyle behaviors such as physical activity, food consumption, sedentary behavior, sleep, and measures of higher order characteristics which directly measured body mass or adiposity (Katzmarzyk, Barreira, Broyles, Champagne, Chaput, Fogelholm, & Lambert, 2013). According to Daniels, Arnett, and Eckel (2005), overweight and/or obese which are influenced by physical inactivity and poor diet, can increase one's risk for diabetes, high blood pressure, high cholesterol, asthma, arthritis, and poor health status.

Physical activity is a very important element in promoting health during childhood but little information is available with regards to physical activity patterns of children during the day at early childhood (Torres-Luque, Beltrán, Calahorro, López-Fernández, & Nikolaidis, 2016). This is consistent with small amount of knowledge in existence with the health of children with developmental disabilities. Children with developmental disabilities are significantly more likely than children without disabilities to die before the age of 17 and have respiratory illness, diabetes and injury-related hospitalizations. Furthermore, children with disabilities also have significantly higher average numbers of ambulatory physician visits and higher rates of continuity of care (Shooshtari, Brownell, Mills, Dik, Yu, Chateau, & Wetzel, 2016).

Individuals with intellectual disabilities experience considerable amounts of health problems compared with the general population, as found in a review of 25 relevant published studies between February 2002 and 2012 covering health promotion and intellectual disabilities (Naaldenberg, Kuijken, van Dooren, & de Valk, 2013). The conclusion suggested that methodological weaknesses and inconsistent experiences make it difficult to compare and contrast the results as studies were very diverse and explored a variety of health issues.

Understanding the attitudes of students with disabilities in physical education could possibly open up new paths in addressing the unique needs for this population. There is a constant debate regarding the relationship between disability and healthy lifestyles in childhood and adolescence. Since a high proportion of disabled children and adolescents are overweight or obese, Reinehr, Dobe, Winkel, Schaefer and Hoffman (2010) have suggested effective strategies for preventing and managing obesity for the disabled students. The U.S. Department of Health and Human Services (2008) indicated that regular physical activity in childhood and adolescence improves strength and endurance, helps build healthy bones and muscles, helps control weight, reduces anxiety and stress, increases self-esteem, and may improve blood pressure and cholesterol levels.

Children with intellectual disabilities in the child protection services. An under representation group is the children and adolescents who live in out of home care in the child protection system. This group has distinct mental health disorders, as well as other types of difficulties, including intellectual disability. The results indicate that there are more vulnerability factors in this group of children compared to their peers who still live at home. In particular, a greater likelihood of having parents with a history of mental health and alcoholism and greater frequency of intellectual disability in their mothers. The state of health and well-being of this group of children presenting intellectual disability who live in residential care revealed the existence of greater alterations on the scale of social and thought problems, as well as a greater probability of being referred for treatment and greater use of psychotropic medication (Sainero, del Valle, López, & Bravo, 2013).

Mental health. Researchers specified that prematurity and low birthweight are significant risk factors for mental health problems among children. A search of relevant literature revealed the effects of prematurity and low birthweight (2500 g) on mental health outcomes among US children aged two –17 years (Singh, Kenney, Ghandour, Kogan, & Lu, 2013). The same study suggested the frequency of mental disorders that was 22.9% among children born prematurely, 28.7% among very-low-birth-weight (1500 g) children, and 18.9% among moderately low-birth-weight (1500–2499 g) children, compared with 15.5% in the general child population. Children born prematurely had 61% higher adjusted odds of serious emotional and behavioral problems, 33% higher chances of depression, and 58% higher odds of anxiety, compared to those born full term. This group of children also had 2.3 times higher rate of autism, 2.9 times higher odds of development delay, and 2.7 times higher likelihood of intellectual disability than term children. In children with very low birthweight 3.2 times higher chances of autism, 1.7 times higher odds of Attention Deficit Disorder Attention/Deficit Hyperactivity Disorder (ADD/ ADHD), 5.4 times higher odds of development delay, and 4.4 times higher odds of intellectual disability than normal birthweight children were observed.

Physical activity not only targets physical but also mental health. A small significant overall effect for physical activity on depression existed. However according to the report more outcome focused that high quality trials are required to effectively inform the implementation of programs to reduce depressive symptoms in children and adolescents (Brown, Pearson, Braithwaite, Brown, & Biddle, 2013). Children identified at age four-five years as having intellectual disability or borderline intellectual functioning, when compared to typically developed children, showed significantly higher rates of possible mental health problems (Emerson, Einfeld, & Stancliffe, 2010).

One area of mental health is social inclusion (Wright, & Stickley, 2013; Llewellyn, Emerson, Honey, & Kariuki, 2013). Although the promotion of social inclusion through sports has received increased attention with other disadvantaged groups. This statement is not the case for children and adults with intellectual disability who experience social isolation (McConkey, Dowling, Hassan, & Menke, 2013). The researchers concluded that unified sports can provide a vehicle for promoting the social inclusion of people with intellectual disabilities. While legislative solutions are common to provide an important framework to support social inclusion, research shows that their full implementation remains problematic. In the context of the current human rights and evidence-based health paradigms, systematic evidence is needed to support efforts to promote social inclusion for people with mental disabilities, highlight social inequities, and develop best practice approaches (Cobigo & Stuart, 2010).

Role of parents' attitude. Based on research findings, educational level and degree of parents are not influential on their attitude towards movement and sport; in addition to no significant relationship between parents' attitude and their physical education participation and gender (Shajie, Raoof, Nayerabadi, & Houshyar, 2014). The study aimed to examine the role of parents' attitudes toward physical activity and sports participation of their school aged children. A short form of attitude questionnaire toward physical activity with 36 questions was randomly administrated to 210 parents. Conversely, the result showed that there was significant difference between parents' attitude toward physical education in motor activity subscale with small amount of separate of active, hyperactive and inactive students.

Barriers of school age children specified that children with disabilities participate less frequently in physical activities, remain less involved, and have less environmental support in the community than children without disabilities. Nevertheless, parents of children with disabilities desired more change in their child's participation than parents of children without disabilities (Bedell, Coster, Law, Liljenquist, Kao, Teplicky, & Khetani, 2013). In the study, parents (N=576) reported on their children aged five to 17 years with disabilities (n=282) and without disabilities (n=294).

The two areas where parents of children with disabilities most frequently desired change were in "unstructured physical activities" and "getting together with other children." The major differences in environmental impact were in physical, social, and cognitive activity demands and availability adequacy of programs and services.

Lack of participation in Physical education class. When compared to typically developed peers, children with an intellectual disability participate in fewer physical activities and skill based activities but participate in more recreational activities, social activities at home and more activities alone (King, Shields, Imms, Black, & Ardern, 2013). These differences are perhaps due to reduced physical, cognitive, and social skills in children with intellectual disability or a lack of supportive environments. In a systematic review, measures of physical activity in children with intellectual disability were undertaken by Hinckson and Curtis (2013). The review identified a clear deficiency in the number of validity and reliability studies used to quantify physical activity in children with intellectual disabilities. Future studies should focus on determining the validity and reliability used of physical activity in children with intellectual disability.

Health risks. Many researchers have documented various health risks for children with developmental disabilities (Schieve, Gonzalez, Boulet, Visser, Rice, Braun, & Boyle, 2012; Shooshtari's et al., 2016). Based on the empirical evidence of the studies provided, children with developmental disabilities may require increased pediatric health care and specialist services, both for their core functional deficits and concurrent medical conditions. Additionally, family support and a love attitude have correlation with health well-being (Wu, Chou, Chen, & Tu, 2016).

In a study by Harvey, Reid, Bloom, Staples, Grizenko, Mbekou, and Joober, (2009), students with emotional and behavioral disabilities often demonstrated poor interactions with peers in physical education class. The same interaction problems were seen with students with attention disorder and lower levels of coordination (Cote, Barker, & Abernathy, 2003). These two indications may be very significant reasons for the negative attitude of students in physical education class which leads to a sedentary lifestyle.

Physical Education and Hidden Disabilities

Many children may have difficulties with reading, writing, or other learning-related tasks at some point, but this does not indicate that these children suffer from learning disabilities. A child with a learning disability often has several related signs, and these persist over time. The footprints of learning disabilities vary from person to person. Common signs that a person may have learning disabilities include the following: (a) difficulty with reading and/or writing, (b) problems with math skills, (c) difficulty remembering, (d) problems paying attention, (e) trouble following directions, (f) poor coordination, (g) difficulty with concepts related to time, and (h) problems staying organized (Eunice Kennedy Shriver National Institute of Child Health and Human Development, 2014).

Some students have disabling conditions that are not visible. The impact of disabilities on children in sport has received relatively little attention, with even less focus on those disabilities that are "hidden" and not physically apparent (Braun & Braun, 2015). The communal hidden or not visible disabilities include attention deficit/hyperactivity disorders (Beyer, Flores, & Vargas-Tonsing, 2008), learning disabilities (Anastasiou & Kauffman, 2013), and emotional and behavioral disabilities (Cook, Tankersley, & Landrum, 2013). The latest results from literature suggest attitudes toward people with disabilities have become more in a positive over the last few decades (Di Nardo, Kudláček, Tafuri, & Sklenaříková, 2014).

Students with physical disabilities frequently have observable physical conditions that influence participation in physical education such as wheelchair use, medical helmets, orthopedics braces, or visual impairments. Many disabling conditions are not externally visible and are referred to as hidden or invisible disabilities. The explosion of the children diagnosed with "invisible disabilities" such as attention deficit hyperactivity disorder, mood and conduct disorders, and high-functioning autism spectrum disorders are seen in recent years (Blum, 2015). Notwithstanding, a condition which may greatly disturb physical education class, children with hidden or invisible disabilities may be treated the same as children without disability.

Individual disability education act (IDEA) lists13 different disability categories under three through 21 year olds. The disability categories include autism, deaf-blindness, deafness, emotional disturbance, hearing impairment, intellectual disability, multiple disabilities, orthopedic impairment, other health impairment, specific learning disability, speech or language impairment, traumatic brain injury, and visual impairment including blindness (National Dissemination Center for Children with Disabilities, 2012). Individual Disability Education Act (IDEA) requires that special education and related services be made available free of charge to every eligible child with a disability, including preschoolers (ages three-21).

Inclusion. Many children with disabilities are placed in an inclusive educational classroom providing students with special needs with education in normal classrooms. Inclusion is the least restrictive educational environment for children with disabilities whereby students are provided the necessary services full time or part time (Gokdere, 2012).

The disproportionate representation of minority students in special education has been a concern for decades (Zhang, Katsiyannis, Ju, & Roberts, 2014). The educational progress of a child assigned to a special education program is expected to be monitored so that reintegration into the regular curriculum is expected. While a number of statistics is used to assess the sufficiency of the program, the disproportionate placement of minority students in special education continues to be a significant and unresolved problem. The Council for Children with Behavioral Disorders (2003) pointed out that CCBD is especially concerned about the overrepresentation of students of color in classes for students with emotional and behavioral disorders, and in more restrictive placements. In this section discussion on: a) learning disabilities, b) emotional/behavioral disabilities, and c) attention deficient with and without hyperactivity disorder will continue as they relate to physical education.

a) **Learning disabilities.** The Individuals with Disability Education Act (IDEA) replaced the Education for All Handicapped Children Act (EHA) when the United States Congress reauthorized All Handicapped Children Act (EHA) and changed the title to IDEA. The goal of Individuals with Disability Education Act (IDEA) is to provide each child with disabilities the same educational opportunities as those students who do not have a disability. Individuals with Disability Education Act (IDEA) is composed of four parts; the main two are part A and part B (Hulett, 2009). Part A of the document is composed of general provisions and part B which is the most important part is assistance for education of all children with disabilities (Center for Parent Information and Resources, 2016). However each part of the law has remained largely the same since the original enactment in 1975. Throughout the years Individuals with Disability Education Act (IDEA) has reauthorized the components of its laws and they have become key concepts of education in regards to children with disabilities (US Department of Education, nd). According to the definition, the specific learning disability is defined as a disorder in one or more of the basic psychological processes involved in understanding or in using language, spoken or written, which disorder may manifest itself in the imperfect ability to listen, think, speak, read, write, spell, or do mathematical calculations (US Department of Education, 2004).

The definition of a learning disability does not include physical or motor difficulties as part of its definition. However, problems with coordination have been historically associated with learning disabilities (Harvey & Reid, 2003). Children with Developmental Coordination Disorder (DCD) and with Attention Deficit/ Hyperactivity Disorder (ADHD) have significantly higher levels of psychological distress such as depression and anxiety than Typical Developing (TD) children, which affects their learning (Missiuna, Cairney, Pollock, Campbell, Russell, Macdonald, & Cousins, 2014).

Chiviacowsky et al. (2013) examined whether the learning benefits of an external focus of attention on the movement effect is related to an internal focus on the movement. This movement was found previously in non-disabled children and adults and if it would also be found in children with intellectual disabilities. The findings concluded that instructions which brought an external focus of attention can improve motor learning in children with learning disabilities.

Learning disabilities can be interrelated in different subjects. A mild developmental delay in visual perception, visual-motor integration and fine motor coordination, and a severe delay in motor skills were found in children with Mathematical Learning Disability (MLD) (Pieters, Desoete, Roeyers, Vanderswalmen, & Van Waelvelde, 2012). Nevertheless, the results found that not all children with Mathematical Learning Disability (MLD) have problems on these domains.

Children with Specific Language Impairments (SLIs) show impaired perception and production of spoken language. These children can also present with motor, auditory, and phonological difficulties (Cumming, Wilson, & Goswami, 2015). Therefore, this population may not understand a rule or directions given in class as their processing deficits make it difficult to follow.

Bullying was reported more than occasionally with special needs children as compared to their peers, but this effect disappeared when behavioral and emotional difficulties were controlled (Fink, Deighton, Humphrey, & Wolpert, 2015). This concept addressed social needs within the physical education context. Adventure Based Learning (ABL), which is a type of curriculum that uses teambuilding activities to promote social skills, (Cosgriff, 2000) should be used in physical education class from early ages to develop a solid base of social development (Samalot-Rivera & Porretta, 2012).

b) Emotional behavioral disabilities. This type of disability impacts a child's ability to function socially, academically, and emotionally as students with emotional and behavioral disabilities often have severe difficulties with emotions, concentration, and behavior (Merikangas & He, 2014). The Individuals with Disabilities Education Act (IDEA) of 2004 characterizes the group of disabilities as Emotional Disturbance (ED). However the term is controversial as it may discriminate against students with behavior issues. As defined by Individuals with Disabilities Education Act (IDEA), emotional disturbance includes schizophrenia but does not apply to children who are socially maladjusted, unless it is determined that they have an emotional disturbance (Code of Federal Regulations, 2004). According to the Center for Disease Control (CDC) approximately 8.3 million children (14.5%) aged four–17 years have parents who have spoken with a health care provider or school staff about the child's emotional or behavioral difficulties (Simpson, Cohen, Pastor, & Reuben, 2008).

Emotional disturbance is a commonly used umbrella term for several different mental disorders such as; anxiety disorder, bipolar disorder, conduct disorder, eating disorder, obsessive-compulsive disorder, and psychotic disorder. According to the Anxiety Disorders Association of America (2010), anxiety disorders are the most common psychiatric illnesses affecting children and adults. This illness is highly treatable but only about 1/3 of those affected receive treatment. A great deal of research is conducted but to date, researchers have not found that any of these factors are the direct cause of behavioral or emotional problems (Council for Exceptional Children, 2015). Equally, no specific research exists linking emotional behavior to motor skills.

Some Black students in disadvantaged districts are emotionally disturbed and many find themselves placed in special education classes. It is confirmed by Chute (2010) that Black students were nearly three times as likely as other students—more than three times as likely as White students—to be identified as having an emotional disturbance. In an alternative study, Mandell, Davis, Bevans, and Guevara (2008) explained: ". . . we hypothesized that when controlling for clinical and service characteristics, we would find that Black children would be more likely than White children to be given the ED (Emotional Disturbance) label" (para. 3).

All emotionally behavioral disabilities, except eating disorders, effect performance in physical education. A large body of research exists regarding methods to provide students with positive behavioral support in the school environment. Federal law mandates that physical education be provided to students with disabilities and defines physical education as the development of physical and motor skills, fundamental motor skills and patterns such as throwing, catching, walking, running, and skills in aquatics, dance, and individual and group games and sports including intramural and lifetime sports (Adapted physical education standards, 2008).

Bingham, Boddy, Ridgers, and Stratton (2015) studied 25 children (aged 11.16 ± 2.37) by monitoring their physical activity over a seven day period. Special needs participants were categorized as autistic, behavioral and emotional needs, or any other health impairment. Behavioral and emotional needs children (65.55 min ± 20.50) were more active than autistic children (43.40 minutes ± 27.50). Children with autism spent more time playing alone and less time in groups than the behavioral and emotional needs children and other health impaired groups (p≤ 0.05). Physical activity levels and play behaviors differ by special need students. Only three children met physical activity guidelines, with all three diagnosed with behavioral and emotional needs.

Fifteen types of training machines were used to investigate the effectiveness of inner muscles and improved abilities to maintain standing posture and walking movements in children with intellectual disabilities. Body control ability was improved over the training period. A significant improvement was observed in the 50-m dash, mean 10-m walk time, and 10-m obstacle course walk (Hayakawa, & Kobayashi, 2011). As results indicated exercise improve and progress movements, which is an indication why children with disabilities need to be active.

Studies typically test a single benefit hypothesized to be associated with physical education such as body mass index. This is while excluding other issues as social skills and not controlling for important confounds such as diet (Simms, Bock, & Hackett, 2013). Therefore if an emotional and/or behavioral disability impact a person's ability to effectively control, recognize, express, and interpret fundamental emotions, it can cause a great social disturbance especially in physical education. Social skills are especially important for transition to school and early school performance which are developed between the ages of three to five. The most suitable subjects for teaching social skills could be physical education (Gregoriadis, Grammatikopoulos, & Zachopoulou, 2013).

A multi-component social skills program including physical education (Van Vugt, Deković, Prinzie, Stams, & Asscher, 2013) was used to evaluate a group based training program. This training program, in social skills, was designed to reduce problem behaviors in (*N* = 161) children between seven and 13 years of age. After a year of follow up, a subsample of the experimental group of children who followed a continuation camp showed large positive changes for all outcome measures, except for externalizing problems which showed a small effect. One year later, positive changes were still evident in the experimental group. Results suggested that more teachers' training and professional development are needed in this area of classroom management with children suffering emotional and behavioral disabilities.

c) **Attention deficit with and without hyperactivity disorder.** Attention-Deficit/Hyperactivity Disorder (ADHD) is a brain disorder marked by an ongoing pattern of inattention and/or hyperactivity-impulsivity that interferes with functioning or development (National Institute of Mental Health, 2016). It is one of the most prevalent mental health disorders of childhood (Lawton, Gerdes, Haack, & Schneider, 2014) which can profoundly affect the academic achievement, well-being, and social interactions of children (ATTENTION-DEFICIT, S. O. 2011). Students with attention disorders cannot benefit from instructions and are often easily distracted. These students cannot dedicate sufficient attention to directions. Previous studies have identified significant inconsistencies in the diagnosis and treatment of Attention Deficit/Hyperactivity Disorder (ADHD), despite increasing rates of prevalence worldwide (Polanczyk, Willcutt, Salum, Kieling, & Rohde, 2014).

An increasing number of studies suggest that physical activity can relieve symptoms of (Attention Deficit/Hyperactivity Disorder) ADHD in children (Berger, Müller, Brähler, Philipsen, & de Zwaan, 2014). Abstract evidence supports the beneficial effects of physical activity on cognitive performance; however, limited research has explored physical activity as a means of managing behavior for students with of Attention Deficit/Hyperactivity Disorder (ADHD) (Gapin, Labban, & Etnier, 2011). Following a single 20-minute session of exercise, with Attention Deficit/Hyperactivity Disorder (ADHD) students and healthy children, match control children exhibited greater response accuracy and stimulus-related processing. Children with Attention Deficit/Hyperactivity Disorder (ADHD) also exhibit selective enhancements in regulatory processes compared with after a similar duration of seated reading (Pontifex, Saliba, Raine, Picchiatti, & Hillman, 2013). In addition, greater performance in the areas of reading and arithmetic were observed following exercise in both groups. The results suggested that single sessions of moderately-intense aerobic exercise may have positive implications for aspects of neurocognitive function and inhibitory control in children with Attention Deficit/ Hyperactivity Disorder (ADHD).

The number of professional athletes who have Attention Deficit/Hyperactivity Disorder (ADHD) is extraordinary, with an estimated eight to 10% of all pro athletes having the condition, as compared to four to five percent of the general population (Dutton, 2016). Many experts suggest a connection between Attention Deficit/ Hyperactivity Disorder (ADHD) and athletics is not a liability to athletics, but rather an asset that can be developed, as having Attention Deficit Disorder (ADD) can actually be an advantage in certain sports (Stabeno, 2004). Thus, physical education and sports play a significant role in children with Attention Deficit/ Hyperactivity Disorder (ADHD). A positive attitude toward physical education can be highly effective in academics and upbringing of the children.

Teachers' Perspective

As schools across the country struggle with new approaches to teacher standards, training, evaluation, development and compensation, teachers' perspectives are considered critical. Moreover, little is known about the opinions, perspectives and perceptions of teachers. Educational programs are built upon the finest practitioners and teachers who have positive attitudes toward inclusion. These programs are more likely to meet the needs of students with developmental disabilities (Hutchinson's et al., 2015). Different perspectives confirm that these teachers have to understand the challenges faced by students with disabilities (Buchanan, Prescott, Schuck, Aubusson, Burke, & Louviere, 2013). Thus, understanding the perspectives of teachers is crucial in educational research. Policies of inclusion in schools now transcend to national boundaries. Yet, less is known about how teachers interact best with each other to establish a successful inclusion environment (Boyle, Topping, Jindal-Snape & Norwich, 2012).

Teachers' perspectives of students' attitude. Investigating the determinants of teachers' perspective of student attitude is import for improving teaching practices. Nonetheless, the role of teaching staff in the promotion of inclusion and the level of specificity in relation to variables which may influence attitudes and behavior need further studies (MacFarlane & Woolfson, 2013).

Teachers' input is required for positive benefits and program outcome (Pence & Dymond, 2016) therefore, responses from teachers regarding the participation of students with disabilities are mostly valued. In a study of teachers' perceptions, DuPaul and Jimerson (2014) reported that students with attention-deficit/hyperactivity disorder (ADHD) exhibited chronic behavior difficulties that deleteriously impacted their academic and social functioning in school settings. As a result of this study, school psychologists were provided with specific directions for advocacy and service delivery that would improve school outcomes for students with attention-deficit/hyperactivity disorder (ADHD).

Teachers' perceptions of children with disabilities in physical education. To explore perceptions of teachers to include children with special needs Morley, Bailey, Tan, and Cooke (2005) used a purposive sample of 43 secondary school (pupils aged 11-18) special educational needs and/or disabled in mainstream physical education. Findings suggested that teachers' conceptions of inclusion are based primarily on the level of children's participation with special educational needs and/or disabilities. This could be affected by the activity area, level of support, and training opportunities available.

To explore teachers' perspectives of barriers and facilitators to physical activity including enabling, reinforcing, and inclining factors amongst children and young people with intellectual disabilities, Downs, Knowles, Fairclough, Heffernan, Whitehead, Halliwell, and Boddy (2014) utilized semi-structured focus groups to explore physical activity of children and young people with intellectual disabilities. Participants were 23 (nine male) teachers and teaching assistants, from three special educational needs schools (1 = Primary, 2 = Secondary) placed in three and focus groups. Findings suggested that students with intellectual disabilities enjoy engaging in physical activity, particularly activities that are of a fun and unstructured nature which allowed for progression of skills and promote independence.

Teachers who were participating in the study recognized that parents and themselves had an influence on children and young people's physical activity engagement. Similar to previous research, teachers documented that children and young adults with an intellectual disability had a lack of understanding on the importance of physical activity engagement and its benefits to health. The research suggested that there is a need for a strong home and school link for children and young adults within special educational needs. The school and home link could prove a key facilitator for active and healthy lifestyles.

Teacher's attitudes towards teaching students with intellectual disabilities was explored in a study by Özer, Nalbant, Ağlamış, Baran, Kaya Samut, Aktop, and Hutzler (2013). In the study Özer et al. (2013) used a representative sample of secondary school physical education teachers to determine the effects of age, gender, teaching experience, and having an understanding of intellectual disabilities. Participants of this study included 729 secondary school physical education teachers who worked in 81 major cities. The teachers' attitudes towards children with an intellectual disability were evaluated using statistical analysis. No significant effect on factors and total attitude scores of gender and having students with intellectual disability were revealed. However significant effects on factors and total attitudes score were found in teaching experiences. Researchers encouraged further development in professional development education programs of adapted physical activity for physical education teachers.

Physical education teachers are faced with many challenges while teaching students with severe intellectual disabilities. The challenges are due to the need for extensive adaptations and assistance with this population. In a study of physical education teachers, Klaviņa, and Strazdiņa (2015) analyzed the attitude of physical education teachers, teaching students with severe intellectual disabilities in the special education environment. The participants included 84 physical education teachers from special schools. Results revealed significant differences across teachers' age, gender and work experience.

In-service teachers. It is recommended that teacher preparation training should include physical education for special education programs for future teachers. In an investigation Tindall, MacDonald, Carroll, and Moody (2014) examined the impact of a 10-week adapted physical activity program on the attitudes and perceptions of 64 pre-service teachers (aged 19–25). In this study, teachers' perceptions of teaching children and young adults with physical, intellectual, and learning disabilities were explored.

A positive change in attitude and perception toward both the idea of inclusion and working with persons with disabilities were reported. Specifically, the in-service teachers' anxieties were diminished and confidence was increased. Most importantly, benefits of the program design, including a combination of theory and practice, were realized. The study findings supported the continued implementation of this type of "live" learning experience as an integral part of physical education preliminary teacher education programming.

Summary

Over the past several decades, attitudes of students toward physical education have been studied and the body of literature and has grown increasingly popular over the past 20 years (Block & Obrusnikova, 2007). Thus far, research is limited and weak with concern to children with hidden or invisible disabilities (Swanson & Harris, 2013). The influences of attitude on children with visible disabilities are well documented in the literature. Nevertheless, findings on students with learning disabilities implied that further attempts were needed for appropriate and accurate research studies. There is a lack of clear research associated with attitude. Further studies to discover ways in which students' attitudes toward physical education and activity impact the behavior is needed in acceleration.

Students who have mild or moderate disabilities such as mild intellectual disability, learning disabilities, and emotional and behavioral disorders are generally placed into general physical education (GPE) classes without an accompanying teacher's aide (Obrusnikova, 2008). The inclusion of students with disabilities into general physical education (GPE) classes has provided a tremendous challenge to physical educators who have planned to meet the physical education needs of children with disabilities, without neglecting the physical education needs of mainstream students (Combs, Elliott, & Whipple, 2010).

In a study (Wang, Wang, & Wen, 2015) examined the teaching behavior of physical education teachers in teaching students with special needs and the factors that determine their teaching behavior. Results revealed that four of five participants interacted more verbally and less physically with students of special needs. To enhance the learning of students with special needs peer partners were used. The modification of instructions and equipment for students with special needs were observed with only two teachers. In occasions, children of special needs were excluded from cooperative activities.

Research suggests (Campos, Ferreira, & Block, 2015) that physical education teachers advocate for inclusion and points out to advantages for students with and without disabilities. Although challenges were raised as obstacles to effectiveness, including the lack of specific training and experience in types and severity of the students' impairments.

Physical education teachers with actual previous experience of teaching pupils with physical disabilities were slightly more positive to inclusive physical education. Teachers play a decisive role in making inclusive education a reality. The particular case of inclusion in physical education poses a specific challenge to teaching practices. Teachers' approaches used to view inclusion may provide special insights into teachers' general attitudes toward inclusion and inclusive practices in the general school curriculum. (Jerlinder, Danermark, & Gill, 2010).

Based on research, children in the integrated setting had significantly more positive attitudes toward peers with behavioral disabilities than those in the segregated setting, but the reverse was true toward peers with physical disabilities (Tripp, French, & Sherrill, 1995).

The aim of physical education teachers is to encourage students to remain active during their lives. Continued physical participation during adulthood have been found to be correlated with positive and satisfying experiences during childhood and adolescence (Eime,Young, Harvey, Charity, & Payne, 2013; Kimiecik, & Horn, 2016). One way of understanding the distinctive physical education needs for students with learning disabilities is to explore this populations' attitude in hopes that policy makers devote closer attention to this field.

Few studies of attitudes toward physical education involving students with disabilities were found in the literature. Investigations of attitudes toward physical education have focused primarily on the perspectives of physical education teachers or nondisabled students participating in physical education classes that include students with disabilities, rather than on the perspectives of students with disabilities themselves. The Restrictions of Institutional Review Board (IRB) and laws protecting students with disabilities create uneasy situations to obtain permission approval for this population.

Chapter 3

Research Method

Physical activity positively affects the health and educational performance of students as studies have confirmed and supported (Fox, Barr-Anderson, Neumark-Sztainer, & Wall, 2010). According to research and governmental documents, students with disabilities engage in less physical activity either in physical education class (Council on Sports Medicine and Fitness & Council on School Health, 2006; U.S. Government Accountability Office, 2010) or recess (Pan, Liu, Chung, & Hsu, 2015) than their nondisabled peers. Overall physical activity of children is low, and the physical inactivity problem is highest in deprived neighborhoods (Flaes, Chinapaw, Koolhaas, van Mechelen, & Verhagen, 2015). In spite of this, there is a strong scientific indication that better academic performance is associated with a higher allocation of time to scheduled exercise in school-age children (Burrows, Correa, & Ibaceta, 2014). However, there is little or no data to justify a common myth that physical education should be reduced or eliminated so children have more time to focus on other subjects (Spark, 2014).

The purpose of this qualitative case study was to understand the perceptions of physical education teachers and their experiences with learning disabled students in their classes. More specifically, this research filled the gap in the literature about attitudes that learning disabled students have on physical education in school. Using teachers' perceptions, this study was designed to inform future practice related to teaching of physical education of students with learning disabilities

Teachers' perceptions of learning disabled students' attitudes toward participation in physical education were assessed through semi-structured interviews of teachers. This chapter begins with a discussion on research methods and designs, followed by sample, material and instruments, data collection, processing and analysis, assumptions, limitations, delimitations and discussion of ethical assurance before summary.

The intent of qualitative research is to understand and explore the complexities of a particular social setting, situation, event, group, or interaction (Creswell et al., 2012). As a result, a qualitative method was chosen to provide tools for the researcher to investigate the phenomenon. The occurrence was within its real-life in an educational setting context and based on several factors; a) the research addressed "what" and "how" questions, b) information was collected without changing the environment, and c) information obtained was about the naturally occurring setting. This method was the most suitable for the study.

Case study was used to describe the phenomenon and the real-life context in which it occurred (Thomas, 2015). Previously, in a similar study Thomas et al., (2011) confirmed that case studies are analyses of persons, events, decisions, periods, projects, policies, institutions, or other systems that are studied holistically by one or more methods. This method of research examines in depth purposive samples to better understand a phenomenon (Yin, 2013). Nonetheless, smaller but focused samples are more often used than large samples which may also be conducted by the same or related researchers or research centers (Denscombe, 2014). In this case study, the occurrence subject of the inquiry which provided an analytical framework was illuminated. In addition, specific information was related to attitude of children with learning disabilities towards physical education. The phenomenon was completed using a rich, descriptive detailed qualitative case study.

Throughout the entire qualitative process the researcher's main objective was to maintain focus on the meaning which the participants hold about the problem or issue (Creswell, 2013). In this case study the problem was that attitude of learning disabled toward participation in physical education class therefore the focus had to maintain on the issue. After collection, the data was analyzed and a summary of findings were concluded. The following questions were used to guide the study:

Q 1. What are physical education teachers' perceptions and experiences in working with learning disabled students in their classes with respect to enjoyment and usefulness attitude components?

Q 2. How would physical education teachers describe the attitudes and behaviors of learning disabled students in their classrooms?

Research Method and Design

Educational research is defined and explained by Gay, Mills, and Airasian (2011) as a formal and systematic application of the scientific method to study the educational problems. The intention of educational research is essentially the same as the goal of all sciences: to describe, explain, predict, or control phenomena- in this case it was educational phenomena. The proposed qualitative research case study was to understand the perceptions of physical education teachers and their experiences with learning disabled students in their classes. The study utilized teachers' perceptions and suggested strategies to help and inform future practices related to teaching of physical education to students with learning disabilities. Teachers' perceptions of these students' attitudes toward participation in physical education was assessed through semi-structured interviews of teachers. The research process remained flexible in order to gather the most data, which allowed for optimal understanding and effective interpretation of the classroom's reality environment (Stake, 2010; Yin et al., 2011).

Examining situational complexity is a vital part of social and behavioral science research (Stake, 2013). Case study research excels to bring an understanding of a complex issue or object and can extend experience or add strength to what is already known through previous research. Emphasize is on detailed contextual analysis of a limited number of participants (Soy, 2015). A research approach with an emphasis on the collection and analysis of quantifiable data is required (Clark & Creswell, 2011). Consequently this study investigated strategies in assisting teachers with learning disabled students to improve their attitude in participation of physical education. In order to determine and understand the experiences and insights of physical education teachers, two proposed research questions were investigated. The participants were provided the opportunity to explain their viewpoints and experiences.

A case study allows for the evaluation of a specific set of actions within the organization in order to understand the implications of those actions (Thomas et al., 2011). The suggested case study evaluated the data and provided insights. These insights analyzed what physical education teachers' perceptions and experiences are in educating learning disabled students in their classes. This study was completed with respect to enjoyment and usefulness components of attitude. The study also concluded how physical education teachers described the attitudes and behaviors of learning disabled students in their classrooms.

As the study relied on qualitative inquiry to capture perspectives and in-depth description from individual participants, it organized around the assumptions of the constructivist worldview (Teddlie & Tashakkori, 2009). Use of qualitative research method allows the researcher to understand the elements, explore themes, and discover the nature of the process (Yin et al., 2011). Thus, interviews were utilized as the method of qualitative data collection to give participants an opportunity to provide their own explanations and reflections (Roulston et al., 2010).

Population

The proposed state is one of the few states that offers physical education mandate in its core curriculum standard. The mandate N.J.S.A.18A:35-8 (1967) which is part of the State's (2012) curriculum and instruction on comprehensive physical education indicates, "The time devoted to such courses shall aggregate at least two and one-half hours in each school week, or proportionately less when holidays fall within the week" (para 2). This is a great opportunity for students to appreciate the physical education as many other states do not offer this course as core curriculum.

A natural setting of qualitative research data collection is where participants experience the problem or issue. The information is gathered by talking directly to individuals and seeing them behave and act within the context (Creswell et al, 2012). Hereafter, the settings of this case study was a district in Northeast of the United States that has a high percentage of African American students, low achievement scores on state mandated tests, and high percentage of students on free or reduced lunch (US News and World Report et al, 2013). This district is a comprehensive community public school district serving students in pre-Kindergarten through 12th grade. The district is one of 31 former Abbott districts statewide (State Department of Education, 2009) and classified by the state Department of Education as "District Factor Group," which is the lowest of eight groupings in terms of income. For the purpose of comparing student performance on statewide assessments across demographically similar school districts, District Factor Groups organize districts statewide to allow comparison by common socioeconomic characteristics of the local districts (State Department of Education, 2016).

The focus of this study remained on students who were identified with specific Learning Disabilities (LD), Emotional Behavioral Disabilities (EBD), or Other Health Impairments (OHI) for Attention Difficulties/Hyperactivity Disorder (ADHD) as defined by the Individuals with Disabilities Education Act (IDEA).

The disabilities had been identified, documented, and written into the students' respective Individual Education Plans (IEPs).

Sample

Sampling is central to the practice of qualitative methods, however compared with data collection and analysis its processes have been discussed relatively small (Robinson, 2014). Qualitative researchers are more concerned with the meaning of the data than making a generalized hypothesis; therefore, frequencies are not as important as understanding (Mason, 2010). Hence, the sample sizes can be much smaller compared to quantitative research to reflect on the purpose of the study (Guest, Bunce, & Johnson, 2006). Nevertheless, the qualitative sample size needs to be adequate to ensure that all relevant information is discovered (Morse, 2010). There is no commonly accepted sample size for qualitative studies because the optimal sample depends on the purpose of the study, research questions, and richness of the data (Elo, Kääriäinen, Kanste, Pölkki, Utriainen, & Kyngäs, 2014). As a result, the target sample size for this study included 10 physical education teachers out of 38 physical education teachers from Pre-Kindergarten to twelfth grades. Eighteen physical education teachers teaching students with learning disabilities at self-contained, inclusion or both settings were invited to take a part in this study.

To ensure the reliability and validity of the interviews Seven Stages of Interviewing (Kvale, 1996) thematizing, designing, interviewing, transcribing, analyzing, verifying, and reporting was followed. Frequently, a study based on interviewing travels through different stages from the initial thematizing and design of the study to the actual interviews (Brinkmann, 2014). Depending upon the level of experience qualitative research design can be complicated with a particular type of methodology. Researchers may aspire to grow and expand their knowledge and experiences with qualitative design in order to better utilize diversified research paradigms for future investigations (Turner, 2010).

Qualitative researchers have long made use of many different interview forms. However making the connections between" theory" and" method" is not always easy to follow (Roulston et al., 2010). In contrast, survey research interviewing standardized questions are often posed to seek answers that are open to quantitative procedures (Brinkmann et al., 2014). In an article Skukauskaite, (2012) presents a reflexive analysis of two transcripts of an open-ended interview and argues for transparency in transcribing processes and outcomes. Participants and transcribing of the data are considered the first step in analysis. The accuracy of the transcription plays a role in determining the correctness of the data that are analyzed with a degree of dependability (Stuckey, 2014).

One of the most critical aspects of a qualitative methodology is the need to write analysis which aims to assemble and interpret the information that was collected. Data analysis is a complex and contested part of the qualitative research process, which has received limited theoretical attention (de Casterle, Gastmans, Bryon, & Denier, 2012). At the end of every interview it is essential to review the notes and the tapes to write a report that summarizes and interprets the information obtained (University of Miami, 2016). In this study, after each interview the digital recording was reviewed. In qualitative studies, one important way of establishing validity is to take transcripts or analyzed results back to some of the interview participants and ask if this is really what they meant (Sewell, 2016). By the final stages of qualitative data analysis, it is advisable to organize the data so that general themes can be formulated and reported (London School of Economics, 2016). In this study teachers were very clear on answers given, therefore there was no demand to contact the participants for clarification. Respecting the interview principles and process, the qualitative data collection of this study is ensured to stand reliable, structured, ethical, and valid.

Creating an interview environment in which participants felt comfortable sharing their life experiences with the researcher is an important task (Roulston et al., 2010). At first, participants were asked a few preliminary questions to develop a conventional sense of their teaching career. Followed by ten formal interview questions intended to produce elaborations on attitudes of children with disabilities in physical education setting. These questions were constructed empirically and were evaluated during this quantitative study (Teddlie & Tashakkori et al., 2009). The research questions were invented to, 1) ask physical education teachers' perceptions and experiences in working with learning disabled students in their classes with respect to enjoyment and usefulness attitude components and 2) ask physical education teachers to describe the attitudes and behaviors of learning disabled students in their classrooms.

Personal involvement may introduce researcher emotions and biases into the study (Rubin & Rubin, 2011). Therefore, efforts were made prior and throughout the interview process, to eliminate any personal beliefs and assumptions regarding past and present experiences with physical education and physical activity. No reflective diary of personal thoughts, feelings, and preconceived notions were maintained during interviews. This is to direct researchers to continually examine their own understandings and reactions to set aside preconceived notions and judgments about the phenomenon of study (Moustakas, 1994).

A small, portable digital recording device was utilized to capture all interview data in a digital format. Audio recording of the interviews was identified in the consent letter. Permission to audio tape the participants' interview, was asked to record the session at the start of the interviews. If a participant expressed any concern or discomfort with the audio recording process when asked initially or at any time during the interview, handwritten notes were taken instead (Rubin & Rubin et al., 2005).

Data Collection, Processing and Analysis

Proceeding the district's permission from the Superintendent's office, a request for site permissions were sent to 21 building principals (Appendix C) and ten principals replied with official letters of consent. Following the proper procedures, an application was filed and approved by Northcentral University (NCU) Institutional Review Board (IRB) and the permission was granted to collect the data. The physical educators were identified through the district's email list and letters of recruitment (Appendix B) were sent individually to 18 teachers of ten participating schools, via Northcentral University's e-mail server. The participation in the study was entirely voluntarily however after accepting to be interviewed a consent signature was mandatory. Ten teachers accepted the invitation and consent letters were sent to all 10 teachers through in-house mailing. All signed consent forms were collected prior to the interview with a copy given to each teacher. Participants could decline or withdraw from the study at any time, and would receive instructions on the process from refusing or withdrawing from participation at any time during the research. No teacher refused to be interviewed after responding to the written consent. Nevertheless four teachers did not agree to a digital recording request, therefore as indicated in documents the answers were handwritten. Interview times were scheduled according to availability of both researcher and the proposed teachers. Each interview was executed in less than one hour.

Qualitative data was collected through teacher interviews. Two research questions were explored through personal, one-on one interview sessions with 10 teachers. These research questions were designed to elicit data that would clarify, explain, enhance, and expand on quantitative data obtained. In addition to capture further insights into the constructs associated with this study (Hatch, 2002). In a study at University of Wisconsin (e al., 2014), researchers indicated, "Data Collection is an important aspect of any type of research study. Inaccurate data collection can impact the results of a study and ultimately lead to invalid results" (para1). In traditional models of research, the ideal is to be as objective and detached as possible so not to contaminate the study. In this study, the detachment from the subject was implemented and no extra questions were asked in fear of leading the interviewees. Further, in qualitative research in which the researcher is the primary instrument of data collection, subjectivity and interaction are assumed (Merriam& Tisdell, 2015).

All interviews took place after school and instructional time at the teachers' school buildings except one which the teacher traveled to the researcher's site due to time constraints. The interviews took place in public but in private places convenient for both the teacher and researcher. The example of these locations are classroom, gymnasium, office and teachers' lounge after school with no traffic. Interviews were scheduled with high trustworthiness to carefully exhibit evaluation of a case study research. During personal interviews of 10 physical education teachers, participants were expected to share their personal views, beliefs, and experiences that would present further understanding of attitude of students with learning disabilities in physical education class. Interviews were utilized as a design for data collection to give participants an opportunity to provide their own explanations and reflections (Roulston et al., 2010). The study relied on qualitative inquiry to capture multiple perspectives and in-depth descriptions from individual participants. A semi-structured interview guide allowed flexibility in the manner and order in which questions were asked; this also ensured that all participants were asked the same general questions. The level of comparability across the interview was maintained by this method.

According to van Teijlingen, (2014) semi-structured interviews are best used when the researcher has limited time or one chance to collect data. The interview guide provides clear instructions for interviewers and often precede with observation or unstructured interviewing techniques. This allows researchers to develop a keen understanding of the topic. The semi-structured interview included open-ended questions, which some turned into discussions. The interview process in this study was semi structured based on Turner (et al., 2010) analysis which included: purpose of interview, format of interview, approximate time of interview session, and how responses were recorded and logged so there is clarity for the participants. The interviews were digital recorded and later transcribed and coded for analysis. The recorder was physically located in the interview setting to maximize recording performance and minimize distraction. Explanation for recording the interview was explained verbally (Saunders, 2012) to each physical education teacher.

Questions were prepared ahead of time, which is a benefit of semi-structured interviews according to van Teijlingen (et al., 2014). Semi-structured interviews provide a clear set of instructions for interviewers and can provide reliable data which include open-ended questions. The purpose of the interview and interview format was reviewed with the participant prior to commencement of the interview (Bridge, 2014).

At the data analysis stage following the interview sessions, first all digitally recorded data was transcribed precisely into Microsoft Word at a personal computer which was placed at the researcher's residence at all times. The personal computer was operating under a password known to the researcher only. First, all interview data was personally transcribed, which provided an additional opportunity to become familiar with the data (McMillan & Schumacher, 2014) and ensured confidentiality. Second, all documents were hand coded and data was read multiple times for familiarity with the depth and breadth of content (Patton et al., 2002). Third, at the end of research all transcriptions were transferred to a computer stick and placed at the researcher's residence. All data was deleted from the personal computer and digital recording.

Assumptions

Four primary assumptions were formulated around the design of this research study. First it was assumed that participating physical education teachers would reply to all questions honestly. It was attempted to build a connection with the participant during the individual interview sessions and participant's experience to be understood by the researcher (Bloomberg & Volpe, 2015). Second, it was assumed that teachers could understand and comprehend the interview questions. Third, it was assumed that the teachers followed all directions accompanying the interview and paid attention to the vocabulary. The final assumption was that as the research followed intrinsic case study methods and the data collected would include multiple realities and diversity of teachers' perceptions (Stake et al., 2010).

Limitations

There are three limitations within this study. As the first limitation, the interviews were assumed to be finished in a month; therefore, it was not a longitudinal study and not extended over a long period of time. In this potentially limitation, the findings would not show any trends over an extended period of time. Furthermore, the second limitation was the district's participation. This study occurred within the physical education content area of one school district in Northeast of the United States. The goal was that findings from this study would be beneficial to other districts nationwide and even at an international scale, to inform the lawmakers in areas of special education in physical education.

The final limitation was with the data collection. The teacher-participant interview questions were carefully designed to avoid use of leading questions. The questions were field-tested by three experts and suggested changes were implemented. Nevertheless, provided questions and conducted face-to-face interviews might put limitations on the study. This limitations could be due to possible bias which might influenced the interview interactions and participant responses. Nonetheless the researcher's personal considerations were separated from the session to the best of ability.

Delimitations

Six delimitations were identified with this study. The results of this study could be generalized to: 1) teachers of physical education were invited for the interview to share their views on students with learning disabilities' attitudes, 2) the population conflagration consist of PreKindergarten to twelfth grade physical education teachers who have taught students with learning disabilities, 3) attitude was examined using an interview approach, 4) participants were chosen based on employment within the district, 5) the sample size was 10 qualified physical education teachers, 6) finally, narrowing the research environment to one district confined the data collection to a small manageable sample size.

Ethical Assurances

A case study can provide tremendous insight into a complex situation. This single qualitative case study seek to apply the experiences and perceptions of 10 physical education teachers and add to the body of knowledge. The researcher was the interviewer and the data collector however Creswell (2009) described, a high level of involvement of a researcher could be problematic. Nonetheless due to small size of data this involvement was manageable. A major challenge for researchers is striving for the highest possible quality when rigor, validity, and the perspectives of qualitative research are credibility and trustworthiness (Cope, 2014). In spite of this, the researcher maintained the position of an investigator throughout the study. Reliability and ethical implications in this study stopped the prejudice of the researcher. According to Flick, (2009) credibility of the researcher is very important in qualitative research because of the involvement of data research and collection.

It was assumed that physical education teachers participating in this research answered all interview questions openly and candidly with honestly in their responses. All teachers had access to the district's grading system and special education students were clearly listed for lesson modification purposes. Researcher bias did not influence the interview interactions and participant responses. As personal beliefs and assumptions of researcher regarding special education students in physical education were not shared with teachers prior or during the interview sessions.

Reflection on the justification of governance processes sheds important however contrasting light on the ethics of other forms and context of research (Sheehan, Marti, & Roberts, 2014). Thus, ethical assurance is one of the issues associated with research. Considerations were given to the potential human subjects' implications, therefore seeking approval from Institutional Review Board (IRB) at Northcentral University (NCU) was pursued prior to the commencement of any data collection. The researcher followed all procedures for the code of ethics at Northcentral University (NCU) and pursued required guidelines at the Institutional Review Board (IRB). No financial or supervisory conflicts of interest existed between the teachers and researcher. Therefore, the researcher was adhered to all ethical principles set by the Northcentral University (NCU) and from Institutional Review Board (IRB).

Summary

This proposed qualitative case study was conducted to address the problem with limited research on how teachers perceive and assist students to participate in physical education (Eklund & Tenenbaum et al., 2014). The research specifically examined the two attitude components of enjoyment and usefulness which can influence whether or not a student will regularly engage in and continue to participate in physical education and activities (Subramaniam & Silverman et al., 2007). The teacher's perspective of children with learning disabilities who are at higher risk for decreased participation in physical education class due to their negative attitude (Collins et al., 2012) is not addressed sufficiently. Furthermore, factors associated with students' attitude toward physical education are not fully understood (Mercier's et al., 2016). This study aimed at understanding of physical education teachers' perceptions and their experiences with learning disabled attitudes in their classes. Teachers' perspectives are important as they provide districts with knowledgeable data on how students respond to learning in an active environment (Smith et al., 2012).

The research questions contributed to purpose of the study. The purpose was to understand the perceptions of physical education teachers and their experiences with learning disabled students in their classes. More specifically, this research filled the gap in the literature about attitudes that learning disabled students have about physical education in school setting. Using teachers' perceptions, this study was designed to inform future practice related to teaching of physical education to students with learning disabilities. Teachers' perceptions of these students' attitudes toward participation in physical education was assessed through semi-structured interviews of teachers. Interview techniques were to gather data directly from ten physical education teachers to answer ten interview questions in order to complete two research questions.

The site selection of this study was an urban school district in the Northeast of the United States. After the permission from the district's Superintendent's office, a request for site permissions were sent to 21 building principals which ten principals replied with official letters of consent. Following the proper procedures, an application was filed and approved by Northcentral University (NCU) Institutional Review Board (IRB) and the permission was granted to collect data. The physical educators were identified through the district's email list and letters of recruitment were sent individually to 18 teachers of ten participating schools, via Northcentral University's e-mail server. The participation in the study was entirely voluntarily however after accepting to be interviewed a consent signature was mandatory. Ten physical education teachers participated in the study. Data was collected by qualitative interview sessions followed by transcription of data collected subsequently the transcription was hand coded and finally analyzed toward contribution to body of knowledge.

Optimistically, the current document will direct physical education teachers' awareness in the area of improving physical activity for students with learning disabilities in physical education programs in schools. Prospectively, this study will improve insight for future researchers and for policy holders in identifying the factors associated with the attitudes of students with learning disabilities toward physical activity in physical education class.

Chapter 4

Findings

The purpose of this qualitative case study was to understand the perceptions of physical education teachers and their experiences with learning disabled students in their classes. More specifically, this research filled the gap in the literature about attitudes that learning disabled students have about physical education in school. Using teachers' perceptions, this study was designed to inform future practice related to teaching of physical education to students with learning disabilities. Teachers' perceptions of these students' attitudes toward participation in physical education was assessed through semi-structured interviews of teachers. The purpose of this chapter is to describe qualitative results and provide an analysis of the findings.

After proper permission from the superintendent office, 21 schools with total of 39 physical education teachers were invited to participate in this study. Ten principals officially agreed to interviews of their 18 physical education teachers assigned to proposed schools. Following all respected regulations of Institutional Review Board (IRB) a permission was granted for a data collection. Formally, invitations were sent to all 18 teachers and ten teachers from the intended school corresponded. All 10 teachers were teaching at least for 6 months at the participated district to students with learning disabilities at inclusion, self-contained or both settings. Therefore, population consisted of 10 certified physical education teachers assigned to PreKidergarten-12 physical education classes. Dworkin (2012) indicated that many sources provide guidance that between five and 50 participants is adequate for a qualitative study.

Informed consent was obtained from each participant prior to interview. Semi-structured interviews contained of 10 questions was guided in answering the research questions and data was collected. The sample size was retained small as Romney, Weller, and Batchelder (1986) found small samples to be sufficient for providing complete and accurate information as long as the participants possess a certain degree of expertise about the topic studied.

Throughout the interviews teachers provided insight for understanding of their experiences with learning disabled students in their physical education classes. Sample size increased emphasis in a detailed analysis of each participant (Smith & Osborne, 2007). Participation by all members involved was completely voluntary nevertheless it was essential for all participants who agreed to an interview to sign a consent. All participants' identities and information remained anonymous by a number assigned to each contributor involved. Moreover all school's identities remained anonymous logically.

This chapter begins with the qualitative research proposal that was guided by two research questions. The study was organized and addressed the following related components: (a) the affective component of attitude (enjoyment), (b) the cognitive component of attitude (perceived usefulness), (c) the attitudes and behaviors of learning disabled, and (d) suggested strategies and experience of teachers. The research questions were explored through personal, one-on-one interview sessions using certified physical education teachers. These two research questions were designed to produce data that would clarify, describe, and expand the study in addition to enhance the future studies.

Q 1. What are physical education teachers' perceptions and experiences in working with learning disabled students in their classes with respect to enjoyment and usefulness attitude components?

Q 2. How would physical education teachers describe the attitudes and behaviors of learning disabled students in their classrooms?

The chapter concludes with an evaluation and interpretation of the findings for each research question.

Results

Prior to coding and analysis, all interviews were transcribed. Then narrative contents of transcriptions were repeatedly reviewed for understanding of conversational topics for interest identification in interview questions. With intention of the data coding and qualitative interpretation repeated readings of the material was required. Initial reviews were completed to determine the extent to which participants reported the same or similar, different or altered perspectives.

Following transcription data analysis was completed by manual coding, which is the best way to analyze qualitative data, (Saldaña, 2015) to identify reoccurring themes. Hand coding of raw data was administered to establish preliminary codes pursued by final codes using Microsoft Word. Participants' data were fully coded individually and then configurations were categorized in clusters. Themes were identified by participants' responses and the results were organized according to each of the two research questions. Results include data gathered from interviews with ten physical education teachers. The purposed section describes the data analyses results for the two quantitative research questions.

Out of 10 teachers one taught at grammar school (Pk-K), three were teaching elementary grades (PK to 5th), one teacher was teaching at a middle school (6 to 8) and five were teachers of middle and high school (6 to12). All teachers were teaching total of 360 students with learning disabilities with no teacher teaching a self-contained class by itself. In other words no teacher was teaching solely self-contained. Six teachers were teaching both inclusion and self-contained and four teachers were teaching inclusion classes only. The range of teaching years were from 3 to 44 years with mean at 19.1 year. Teachers were teaching at the proposed district from 3 to 44 years with mean of 17.1 year and at the current school from 3 to 27 years with mean of 13.7 years.

Research Question 1 (Q1)

The first qualitative research question was related specifically to enjoyment and usefulness of physical education for students with disabilities. Specifically, the research question was, "What are physical education teachers' perceptions and experiences in working with learning disabled students in their classes with respect to enjoyment and usefulness attitude components?

The affective component of attitude (enjoyment)

Enjoyment. Five Primary themes emerged as factored related to the enjoyment of physical education for children with disabilities (a) teacher role, (b) role of students with learning disabilities, (c) role of students without disabilities, (d) role of skills, and (e) structure.

Teacher role. Five teachers indicated that to make the activities more enjoyable students had "choices" and "freedom of exploration". Two teachers specified that when students with learning disabilities were chosen as helpers and leaders, they enjoyed their physical education time. While three others directed the focus on "actively engagement", "low age of children" and "the sport itself". Teacher #2 indicated that because her students are very young they all enjoy the physical activities. Whereas teacher #3 said, "I teach swimming and the whole idea of getting in the water is enjoyable. I don't have to do anything except for them to get in the water and explore."

There were a few questions directed to moments when students with learning disabilities did not enjoy physical education class. Two teachers indicated that teachers' assistance is used as students demonstrate "impatient behaviors" or if more explanation is needed. At different levels four teachers posed a common position designated the function of "a facilitator", "a motivator", "a director" and "a conversationalist" effective if signs of displeasure is observed. To endorse the situation, teacher #9 said, "After reviewing the concepts and activity, I monitored the activity to ensure the students were participating safely, following the rules, using proper technique, and provided whole group, small group, and/or individual assistance when needed." Three other teachers all had different claims, "Children do not enjoy physical education class when they do not play" as teacher # 3 statement was supported by teacher #10 statement when said, "I make sure that students with a disability are always included in any game they want to play." A teacher also indicated that his role is very minimal when students do not enjoy physical activities.

Role of students with learning disabilities. Seven teachers accounted that when students with disabilities enjoy the class is once they participate with everyone else with no differentiation between such students vs. students with no learning disabilities. Moreover, two teachers specified that students with learning disabilities were given "leadership roles" in terms of demonstration, "helping other students" or "direct the class". Teacher #1 verbalized that the role is 50/50 and continued, "Some students with disabilities are really good and anxious but some are criers, runners and don't want to stay put therefore those students are problematic."

Once teachers were asked to reflect on times when children with learning disabilities did not enjoy physical education, "sitting on the bench", "laziness", "saying tired", "disinterested", "passive", "lack of participation" emerged from the question and reported by five teachers. Two teachers testified to "Temper tantrums" and "creating a chaotic environment". However, two other teachers conveyed that their students are part of a team therefore they never "feel as though they are not enjoying themselves or not having a good time."

Role of students without learning disabilities. The results were more scattered at this section when enjoyment of students without learning disabilities as it related to students with learning disabilities were examined. Six teachers mentioned that students without disabilities help those who are learning disabled however each teacher had own interpretation of "help". Two teachers indicated that help was by "taking leadership roles". Teacher #2 mentioned helping by, "Mentoring, protecting and watching out for students with disabilities." In addition, two teachers communicated on "companionate buddies" as source of help. Leadership roles of students without disabilities were offered positively by two teachers while two other teachers spoke on participation of all students to incorporate the activities with given each student an "equal opportunity to participate".

In terms of what the roles of students without learning disabilities were when students with learning disabilities disenjoyed the physical activities, six teachers displayed positive behaviors. All these teachers exhibited that their students without disabilities, "draw in" the students with learning disabilities into activities, worked as "mentors", "helped", "encouraged", and all were "members of a team". Although one of the same teachers described that sometimes students without disabilities "push them away but for the most part small number of students were not cooperating with students with disabilities". Two teachers indicated that students in general education will "wait" or "sit" if the activities are not enjoyable. Teacher #7 recounted the helpfulness of students at "some of the time" and one teacher did not answer the question.

Role of skills. The common theme of this piece on enjoyment was that similar activities were matched with or without disabled students while "skill levels and performance have nothing to do with learning disability" as a teacher described it "students are grouped accordingly and some may need assistance" four teachers supported this process. Nevertheless, two teachers contested such practice and replied that students are mixed in with their skill abilities in "heterogeneously" based skill levels. Two teachers corresponded that there is not as much "disparity" when 3-4-5 grades hit the ball. The indication was that one half can and the other half because of emotional issues cannot perform the skill correctly.

Conversely "younger ones" have a "tough time" and sometimes skills plus knowing rules and strategies become difficult in an environment with limited time to explain. This is aligned with Ozmun and Gallahue (2016) disclosing that at the level of reflex inhibition, voluntary movement is poorly differentiated and integrated. One teacher articulated that skill levels play a role but games and lessons can be modified so it can be enjoyed by all levels of abilities. In addition, one of the teachers did not answer the question.

The results on the roles of skill levels when the activities are not enjoyable were extraordinary scattered. Teacher #1 pointed toward the impatient nature of children with learning disabilities when she implied, "For example we are doing shooting and showing hand placement and then, targeting they do not enjoy that, they want to get the ball and go and play. Don't want to listen to explanations or see the demonstration. Like to go and run with it." This notion is associated with many research which signifies children with disabilities are impatient. Jones, Harrison, Harp, and Sheppard-Jones (2016) implied that students with intellectual disability are impatient during group activities.

The statement almost associates with teacher #3's account when was said: "We playing a game. If lesson is not finished, we don't play a game". Therefore there are times when the lessons are not taught the way they are planned. Teacher #8 signaled that the students with learning disabilities possess problems with games' directions. All these three teachers were speaking of a common component problem in the field of physical education which is the short attention span. Students with learning disabilities deserve individual classroom attention and extra time (Cortiella & Horowitz, 2014). The equipment was also mentioned by an elementary teacher that uncomfortable equipment brings unenjoyable experience due to under developed motor skills. One of the teachers explained that since all students are beginners and at pre-control level therefore skills do not produce significant role.

In a conflicting view a highs school teacher presented that skills play a significant role in activities. Moving forward teacher #6 explained that students are grouped together equally based on their skills' abilities but in contrast teacher #9 described that grouping is heterogeneously based on the skill level. Two teachers did not answer the question.

Structure. Teacher #1 indicated, "Activities are structured however special need students are not held accountable exactly to the same structures. There are aids for assistance, and often students are let to explore but aids bring them back in." Nearly all teachers (7) were agreed that when students are enjoying the physical activities such environments were structured. Teacher #9 expressed, "The activities had some structure."

Students were given rules and taught concepts, then required to apply those basic concepts in the activity. This allowed students to move freely in a designated playing area attempting to incorporate what was being taught." An inclusive, structured and supportive environment promotes physical activity engagement in adolescents with intellectual disabilities (Pan, Liu, Chung, & Hsu, 2015). Three teachers believed that children will enjoy physical activities in unstructured settings.

In terms of how structured the activities are when students are not enjoying the physical education, six teachers replied that activities were structured, three talked on semi structured activities. One teacher did not answer while clearly no teacher indicated that activities were not structured.

Finally, the teachers were asked if they could change one thing to make physical education enjoyable for students with learning disabilities, what it would be. The desire of teachers divided into 3 major themes, equipment, facility and time.

Table 1.

Table for Changes to Make Physical Education More Enjoyable.

Topic	Description
Equipment	#4. Equipment, more specific to their needs.
	#10. I personally feel as though the students that we have with disabilities truly enjoy physical education because they are higher functioning although I'm not sure I would be able to say the same if we had lower function students due to lack of resources and equipment.
Facility	#8. A room without distractions so they can focus and stay on me. Make PE shorter for self-contained. It's 40-45min class. Kids are distracted and tired. They need change. Maybe less structure and allow them to be more creative.
	#9. Larger playing area. My school has a small gym with large class sizes, which can make it challenging when trying to get all of the students actively engaged in the activity at once.
Time	#1. Part of me feels it works with inclusion and I would continue that and partner them up. Part of me says maybe bigger self-contained class is better. I had 1st grade self-contained class with 5 students last year, what was I going to do with them? The periods are too long at 40min and you can't keep it going. I'm torn & don't know how to improve it.

#2. I wish I had one period every week that I could spend time just with learning disability students to breakdown the skills and then with the rest for group.

#3. Give them more time. I rather to have them 3 days a week for 50min rather than every day for 40 min. In 40 min they have to change, shower, learn, shower, and change. Even that 10min is a huge advantage. I have them for 10 weeks, 5 days for 40 min but time is an issue.

The cognitive component of attitude (perceived usefulness)

Usefulness. Five Primary themes emerged as factored related to the usefulness of physical education for children with disabilities (a) teacher role, (b) role of students with learning disabilities, (c) role of students without disabilities, (d) role of skills, and (e) structure.

Teacher role. All ten teachers answered this question and elaborated on their role when physical education is useful. Moreover, teachers' interpretation was scattered. Eight of the teachers reported that physical education class is useful due to its "development of lifestyle" which can be used outside of school. Nonetheless unlike examples were used to describe the "lifestyle development". Participants informed that sociability such as sharing and trusting, setting up reasonable goals, taking the leadership role and to be able to speak in public, competitiveness and incorporating strategies are skills which will continue later in life beyond the traditional school experience. One teacher stated that the teacher role is to provide individual attention and progressing on own pace. In addition, another teacher mentioned that physical education is useful due to incorporation of music.

Contributors to the study shared their roles regarding instances when they considered the activities were not useful. In spite of teachers' role three teachers believed that all activities in physical education classes were useful. They reflected that, "I don't find anything not useful" and, "Every activity has usefulness in it."

Among the participants five teachers shared their roles as, "motivator", "entertainer", "reflector", "not controller", "phasing out the activity", "Monitoring the activities", and "self-assessor" when they motioned the activities were not useful. "It's hard when you have so many students in the gym and a total of 7 sections of classes with special education. Sometimes the students with learning disabilities don't understand the rules and procedures of the games or activities which causes more chaos in the gym. Sometimes controlled games are not useful to the students with disabilities because it causes a safety issue within the gym" said teacher # 6. "After reviewing the concepts and activity, I monitor the activity to ensure the students are participating safely, following the rules, using proper technique, and provide whole group, small group, and/or individual assistance when needed" teacher # 9 added. A teacher echoed "small part" as his role and one participant did not respond to the question.

Role of students with learning disabilities. The physical education teachers strongly were agreed on constructive effect of usefulness. All ten teacher homogeneously identified how students "participate" in the class and in what ways students "blend in", "take leadership role" and "love" the class. One teacher explained, "If Johnny can't read, doesn't mean Johnny can't swim."

All participants except two, reported that students with learning disabilities had positive and negative beliefs when they found the activities not useful. On the optimistic note three teachers reported "positive" and "active participation" in addition to "understanding". Although four participants talked on "frustration", "not engaged, focused or participation". Two teachers did not answer the question and one teacher stated a "large role" but did not explain specifically.

Role of students without disabilities. Four teachers found the role of students without disabilities the "same" as students with disabilities. However, two teachers did not mention the same role but referenced "helpful". One teacher mentioned that students without disabilities are "more attentive" while two other teachers indicated "active participation" and "very much."

In relations to the role of students without disabilities when teachers found activities not useful three teachers found the students "unengaged and unfocused" and "inactive" while two teachers reported the "same" role. One teacher confessed that all lessons are useful moreover another teacher reported that children without disabilities verbalize to be engaged in different activities. This is when a different teacher narrated that children without disabilities remain as active participants. Two teachers did not answer the question.

Role of skills. Four teachers reported that at the skill level when they considered activities usefulness the students were "equally" placed in teams or skills were "mixed". A large number of physical activities were toward the "coordination" based on one teachers' testimony. In addition teacher #4 said that students "trying to do the best within the level of ability". Whereas teacher #7 attest to the "large role" skills, additional teacher explained how skills are added every year. Two teachers did not answer the question.

In role of skills stipulation when it was not useful and four teachers found it unnecessary to answer the question. Two teachers reported that in such case students with learning disabilities were "not happy" and claimed the activities are "unfair". As teacher #2 said, "I don't think anything is not useful. Sometimes we try a new activity and it may not work exactly the way we want it. It doesn't mean necessary is not useful. We have to modify for some students but that's for everyone." Other three teachers reported on "small role", "peer to peer instruction" and "phasing out the activity."

Structure. Once activities were useful no teacher reported on unstructured activities. Five teachers reported that the activities are structures, "We have too many students in a gym at once to have any unstructured activities. At times, there is 100 plus students in the gym" a teacher shared. Equally five teachers declared that their activities are semi structured. "It was mixed. Ultimately, the more actively engaged the students were the more beneficial I felt the lesson was for the students in understanding useful concepts being taught" explanation by teacher # 9.

Five teachers confirmed that activities were structured even though the activities might have not been useful. Three teachers reported on semi structured activities. A teacher reported, "In my experience all tools were always useful" and a teacher did not answer the questions.

At the end of this section finally, teachers were asked if they could change one thing to make physical education useful for students with learning disabilities, what it would be. Teachers corroborated 5 different categories of activity, class structure, communication, equipment, facility, and time.

Table 2.

Table for Changes to Make Physical Education More Useful.

Topic	Description
Activity	#2. Not so many team sports or competition because it's intimidating. More fitness.
	#3. Children need to be exposed to different activities whether it's swimming, lacrosse, not to be exposed to kick ball or basketball all the time or even jump rope. They need to be exposed and learn other physical/ educational activities that they may not enjoy but they need to explore and experience more.

Class Structure	#5. Self-contained physical education because it is not much pressure.
	#6. Smaller class size.
Communication	#4. Communication maybe with Child Study Team and engaged with them.
	Equipment #10. Invest in proper special education equipment.
	Facility # 1. Be able to for example play on tennis court or a field as appose to the gym as students don't get a real feel because we are doing drills. And modify things because we are indoor. So exposure to real thing with all the equipment so they get the whole concept.
	Time: #7. I believe having physical education at least 2x a week would be useful.
	#8. More time.

Research Question 2 (Q2)

The second qualitative research question was related specifically to 1) to the attitudes and behaviors of learning disabled and 2) suggested strategies and experiences of teachers in assisting of current physical education teachers and shaping the future of profession. Specifically, the research question asked, "How would physical education teachers describe the attitudes and behaviors of learning disabled students in their classrooms?"

Appropriately, to understand the attitudes and behaviors of learning disabled three interview questions were designed. In response to increase positive attitudes and behavior of students with learning disabilities in physical education three primary themes emerged as factored related to, 1) if students should participate in self-contained physical education which means more restricted environment, 2) if learning disabled students should participate in a non-co-ed class, and 3) if learning disabled suffer from lack of physical activity during the physical education class.

The attitudes and behaviors of learning disabled

Self-contained class. Six teachers reported that inclusion is a suitable setting for such students because they learn positive reinforcements from their peers. The other four teacher could not arise to a concrete answer, they considered the condition of each individual child. Perhaps due to "processing differently" teachers would want to teach the instructions to individuals which is very difficult in physical education setting.

Non-co-ed class. Nine teachers acknowledged that participation in non-co-ed physical education classes are not necessary. Nevertheless, one teacher due to the nature of her own environment and the sport taught indicated that one grade (8) is not co-ed.

Lack of physical education. Seven teachers said that their learning disable students do not suffer from lack of physical activity in physical education class. Conversely two teachers indicated that they have observed lack of physical activity during physical education. Teacher number 6 said: "They are not able to get the most out of P.E under the circumstances in the gym with EX. Large class size." In addition, one teacher answered "yes and no".

Teachers conveyed the factors related to lack of physical activity could relate to activities itself. As teacher #1 testified, "Activities which the students have to wait their turn can turn itself to some students not being physically active enough in my opinion." Teacher #6 who answered positive to lack of physical education responded, "Students with disabilities need the right amount of physical activity in their lives just as regular students do. The students are in the class room all day and when it comes time for gym some of them may sit out or not participate because they feel as if they don't need it."

To comprehend suggested strategies and experiences of teachers in assisting current physical education teachers and shaping the future of profession questions were asked in two interview questions and were developed in two themes, 1) suggestions in helping students with learning disabilities to increase physical activity in physical education class and 2) experiences in helping students with learning disabilities to improve their attitude in physical education participation. Teachers offer details on suggestions and experiences in helping students with learning disabilities to improve attitude in order to increase physical activity in physical education class.

Suggested strategies and experience of teachers

Suggestions. With guidance of experienced physical education teachers all students with learning disabilities can enjoy physical education class. Certain conditions may impair a child's ability to participate in required exercises, movements or sports activities found in the traditional physical education. Under Individual Disability Education Act (IDEA), rather than excluding children with special needs, public schools are required to offer adaptive programs which provide students with special needs, the opportunity to keep their bodies healthy and involve certain adjustments to the standard curriculum.

With assistance from supportive physical education teachers, teacher aides and/or para-educators these students enjoy exercising along with their peers. Finding from a review (Haegele & Sutherland, 2015), the notion that positive attitudes of physical educators may be a critical feature in ensuring meaningful learning experiences for students with disabilities is supported.

Depending on the severity of the disability and the modifications, a child may either participate in a small modified physical education class with other special needs students or in a large mainstream physical education. The suggestions at this section can be functional at both settings. All teachers answered this section enthusiastically and offered suggestions for teachers, students and parents. The 'motivation' had the highest frequency.

Table 3.

Table for Helping Students with Learning Disabilities to Increase Physical Activity in Physical Education Class.

Topic	Suggestions Description
Teachers	Create extra time (maybe lunch time), create fun activities, encouragements, keeping on task, knowing limits, individuality, involvement, make them part of class, maximum participation, modification motivation, no passive words, use teacher assistants, utilize the space, nurture, positive feedback, praise, stick to boundaries, work on coordination, know learning styles.
Students	Follow directions and rules, follow teacher input.
Parents	Have students involved.

Experiences. Teaching experience is positively associated with student achievement. Experience has long been considered the best teacher of knowledge and since we cannot experience everything, other people's experiences become the substitute for better mentoring which really helps the teachers (Siemens, 2014). An opportunity to explore educational experience enable current and future teachers to discover teaching which will help to develop the strong leadership traits found in high-quality educators.

The school experiences of students with disabilities can be positively or negatively influenced by the attitudes and behaviors of students, staff, and by general school policies (Milsom, 2006). Therefor consuming teachers' experiences to improving attitude of students with learning disability is imperative. Partaking a variety of experiences contributed to nine teachers answering this section enthusiastically and offered experiences for teachers, schools, and colleges. The 'encouragement' had the highest frequency.

Table 4.
Table for Helping Students with Learning Disabilities to Improve Their Attitude in Physical Education Class.

Topic	Experience Description
Teachers	Assisting, encouragement, establish positive experience, form a relationship, giving jobs, individualization, introduce variety of sports and activities, make corrections not fixing mistakes, patience, positive reinforcement, proud, smile, tolerance.
Schools	Provide more professional development specifically on children with disabilities.
Colleges	Provide more courses on students with disabilities.

Evaluation of Findings

This section contains a discussion on the meaning of findings from the study. Understanding the issues that influence attitudes toward physical education in Pre-Kindergarten to twelfth grade was design of this study. In this section, the findings of this study are presented in the grounded theory framework. The study was organized around the two components attitudinal theory framework which was characterized by affective (enjoyment) and cognitive (perceived usefulness) components of students with learning disabilities and investigated the suggestions and experiences of teachers. The ten education staff members who were interviewed and participated provided a tremendous amount of rich data in response to the research questions.

Teacher interviews consisted of ten questions and allowed the participants to speak unreservedly about their perception of attitudes and experiences. An evaluation of findings from a qualitative research question associated with perceptions and experiences of teachers in working with learning disabled students in their classes in terms of enjoyment and usefulness is presented first. Followed by an evaluation of findings from a research question associated with the qualitative study of attitudes and behaviors of learning disabled students. Finally, teachers offer details on suggestions and experiences in helping students with learning disabilities to improve attitude in order to increase physical activity in physical education class.

The 1st question guiding this study was:

Research Question 1: Q 1. What are physical education teachers' perceptions and experiences in working with learning disabled students in their classes with respect to enjoyment and usefulness attitude components?

Enjoyment. The first part of this question was characterized by the affective (enjoyment) component of attitude theory. The findings suggested that whether teachers considered students were or were not enjoying the physical activities, there were no perceptible differences on the level of structural components. Overall, the analysis suggests high level of structural level. The current data proposed that most structured physical activities are part of physical education as an important part of the preschool curriculum that provides regular opportunities for physical activity while promoting physical fitness and motor skill development and helping children develop cognitive, social, and emotional skills (Chow, McKenzie, & Louie, 2015). The National Association for Sport and Physical Education (NASPE, 2011) recommends that students should accumulate at least 60 minutes of structured physical activity. Although neither of the two studies mentioned disaggregated data by disability significance in the physical education setting. Recent research indicates that combining structured contact, knowledge acquisition, and awareness activities are effective methods for changing attitudes of disabled (Orlić, Pejčić, Lazarević, & Milanović, 2016; Vaillo, Hutzler, Santiago, & Murcia, 2016).

One explanation for similar levels of structure pertain to enjoyable or not enjoyable physical activity could related to the teacher role at delivery of curricular content. With 19.1 average years of experience physical educators involved in the study seemed skilled in delivering the curriculum. Freedom of exploration and time to experience were dedicated but when the teachers felt that activities were not enjoyable their role became to motivate and redirect the students. The findings of a research (Bennie, Peralta, Gibbons, Lubans, & Rosenkranz, 2016) showed that motivational teaching strategies were acceptable when embedded within certain physical education contexts and each strategy successfully enhanced student physical education, enjoyment, motivation, and student learning. In this differentiated instruction, a wide range of student skills and abilities are appropriately addressed and accommodated. In a similar study (Jaakkola, Wang, Soini, & Liukkonen, 2015) the results showed that the students' perceptions of various motivational climates created differential levels of enjoyment in physical education classes.

Analysis revealed support for the differences in levels of participations toward physical education when students with learning disabilities enjoyed and did not enjoy the activities. Comprehensive examination suggests relatively equivalent role of participation with minimal difference in comparison to non-learning disabled when activities were enjoyable. Similar study proposes school students value fun and enjoyment as attractive and important attributes of physical education (Liu, Wang, & Xu, 2008). Enjoyment component of attitude has been identified as a significant influence on participation (Barr-Anderson, Neumark-Sztainer, Lytle, Schmitz, Ward, Conway, & Pate, 2008; Winnick, & Porretta, 2016). Moreover, interventions should perhaps initially focus on increasing enjoyment of physical activity. Greater physical activity's enjoyment appears to influence individuals' self-reported ability to engage in regular physical activity (Lewis, Williams, Frayeh, & Marcus, 2016). Reportedly children's passive and uninterested attitudes were described by teachers when enjoyment element was absent or vague in activities. Intrinsic importance related to children much more likely to reject chances to engage in activities (SPARK, 2016) was stated. Alternatively, students without disabilities cooperated and uniquely played the roles of mentors to draw encouragement for their disabled peers whether activities were enjoyable or at none enjoyable level.

According to finding the skill levels remained the same for non-disabled students however at times inserting rules and strategies produced more difficult situations. But again rules, which might have considered one form of communicating expectations, may constitute the most cost-effective form of classroom management and play an important role (Bicard, 2000) therefore teachers modified the skills. Physical ability levels have been shown to influence attitude toward physical education (Bernstein, Phillips, & Silverman, 2011). Furthermore, Students with learning disabilities were restless when enjoyment of activities at the skill level were not present however teachers exploited grouping strategies.

Finding from teachers to transform one factor to make physical education more enjoyable for students with learnings disabilities suggests adjustments to facility, time (longer and shorter), and equipment. Implementing or maintaining regular physical education classes have its own challenge including lack of certified staff, inadequate indoor facilities/equipment, and inadequate outdoor facilities which are impacting the state laws and district policies on physical education (Slater, Nicholson, Chriqui, Turner, & Chaloupka, 2012). Significant inattention, hyperactivity, distractibility, or a combination are a brain based disorder for children with Attention Deficit Disorder (ADD) (Cortiella et.al, 2014). Therefore, if students are in an environment of distractions the instruction becomes extremely time consuming and problematic.

The national recommendation for school physical education endorsed by the National Association of Sport and Physical Education (NASPE, 2004) and the American Heart Association (2008) is that elementary school students to be offered at least 150 minutes per week of physical education. Nevertheless, fewer than 20% of third grade students at public elementary schools in the United States were offered this amount during the 2007-2008 school year (Turner, Chaloupka, Chriqui, & Sandoval, 2010).

The time allocated for students with learning disabilities in self-contained class was challenged by teachers especially at the elementary level calling it long for the particular age group. However, inclusion stayed the same but teachers also shared that 40 minutes given in each day is not enough. The time distribution could be longer at a given day but shorter during the week. Although only a few studies have examined the impact of state level policies on the amount of time allocated to physical education and physical activity during the school day, all show an increase in the number of weekly physical education minutes after the passage of a state law (Barroso, Kelder, Springer, Smith, Ranjit, Ledingham, & Hoelscher, 2009; Kelder, Springer, Barroso, Smith, Sanchez, Ranjit, & Hoelscher, 2009). While implementation of state policy varied across the affected school districts some schools cited competing time demands as a barrier to full implementation (Evenson, Ballard, Lee, & Ammerman, 2009).

Readily available are many research conducted in regards to appropriate equipment for students with physical disabilities (Conroy, 2012; Fitzgerald & Stride, 2012; Ballard, 2016; Roth, Zittel, Pyfer, & Auxter, 2016) while there is no sufficient research of equipment for student with learning disabilities. As it was mentioned by a teacher high functioning learning disabled can function with mainstream equipment but there is a demand for further research in the area.

Usefulness. The second part of this question characterized by cognitive (perceived usefulness) component of attitude theory. The interview questions were characterized by the cognitive component of attitude theory. Analysis reveals support for minimal differences in structural levels of perceived usefulness toward physical education. The structured physical education class was implemented whether teachers believed the activities were useful or not useful. Teachers' perceived usefulness in critical reasoning is consistent with previous studies resulting in ensuring continued pursuit of active lifestyle (Centers for Disease Control, 2013), social issues (Holt, 2016), sharing, trusting (Flory & McCaughtry, 2011), and socialization (Rarick, 2012). Few teachers believed that all activities are useful in their physical education while few reflected, self-assessed and at times phased out the activity.

Benefits associated with participation in physical activity have been publicized. All teachers reported on the useful values of physical education in this study and consistency among teachers exited. Children with learning disabilities blended in and accepted the exact role as non-learning disable peer.

The teachers who believed in occasions of non-useful activities reported on lack of insignificant differences between the two groups of students with learning disabilities and mainstream. Both groups showed lack of interest and no participatory, frustration and disruption. These findings are consistent with previous study results (Cothran & Kulinna, 2015) that the students reported using nonparticipation, powerful personality persuasion, disruption in physical education. Perceived usefulness of physical education promotes responsible behavior and motivates success, which leads to less hostility and frustration, and less violent be systematic, flexible, and ever changing based on the needs of each student (Lavay, French, & Henderson, 2015). Consuming opportunity to involve and engage in profound activities would positively intensify students' attitudes toward physical activity.

Once activities were useful students learned more games and strategies by grade level. Similarly, students without disabilities could assist those with learning disabilities through grouping with no dominate person. Students with learning disabilities exhibited low attitudes toward physical education referred to skill levels if usefulness was not present.

Finding from teachers to transform one factor to make physical education more useful for students with learnings disabilities suggests facility, exposure, time, and class size. The facility and time for physical education classes were explained however teachers mentioned real life experiences with activities having a real-world application and universally designed (Davis & Hardin, 2013). Moreover, exposure to many different sports was cited. A study in Singapore suggests that secondary school, youths are encouraged and exposed to many different sports (Michael & Marcus, 2015). Engaging in the same activities during one academic year or throughout years may result in a deficiency of interest, which in turn lowers perception of usefulness. As in many school's students maintain the same physical education teacher for years, activities that are new, unique, and challenging have a positive influence on attitude (Smith & St. Pierre, 2009).

The National Association for Sports and Physical Education (NASPE) recommends that the size of physical education class to be consistent with those of other subject areas for safe and effective instruction. Once students with special needs are included in regular physical education classes, their placement should not cause an appropriate class size to be exceeded (2006). Physical education has evolved from playing recreational games to an environment focused on learning through movement therefore class size has an effect on differentiating instruction to meet the needs of all students (Brabo, 2013).

The 2nd question guiding this study was:

Research Question 2: How would physical education teachers describe the attitudes and behaviors of learning disabled students in their classrooms?

This section is an evaluation of findings from a research question associated with the qualitative study of attitudes and behaviors of learning disabled students. Followed by teachers' suggestions and experiences used for current and future practices. Two interview questions guided this section which were divided into four subdivisions. The questions were designed to understand how to increase positive attitude and behavior of students with learning disabilities in physical education.

Self-contained vs. inclusion. Over the last decade, the idea of students with disabilities and special educational needs in inclusion classes have become increasingly the focus of national and international policies (Doulkeridou, Evaggelinou, Mouratidou, Koidou, Panagiotou, & Kudlacek, 2011). In this study majority of teachers confessed that inclusion is a suitable placement for the current student body. Few teachers have expressed that some lessons and skills are modified which is consistent with a study that said realistic curricular adaptations can make inclusive education successful (Cook, Klein, & Chen, 2015). Students who are eligible for special education are entitled to any accommodations that are necessary to help them access the educational curriculum and meet the goals in their Individual Educational Plans (IEP).

Teachers of inclusion classrooms are entitled to any training and other supports that they require to assist all students in their classrooms (Children's Hospital of Philadelphia, 2016). In low functioning students and those with behavioral disorder, self-contained class is an appropriate environment as teachers shared. Students can participate successfully and the teacher can apply the same plan in the physical education or dance but the student may need to rest physically, reduce stimulation, or relax emotionally (Cone & Cone, 2011). Nevertheless, for students in self-contained classrooms, interaction with typically developing peers during the school day is important (Jones & Hensley, 2012).

Co-ed physical education. The US Department of Education is giving more liberties to school districts in offering single-sex schools in order to adequately serve the needs of students (Blake, 2012). Conversely, uniformly all teachers admitted that all physical education should continue its role in co-educational setting. Nevertheless, a swimming teacher professed that her eighth grade class is single sex and students more readily engaged and connected with activities. The finding affirmed that co-educational physical education at self-contained or inclusion does not possess any difference in attitude on children with learning disabilities. The debate about co-education versus single-sex groups in physical education have been actively studied from a socio-cultural to physical education (Sykes, 2011).

Lack of physical education. The unexpected results were delivered when teachers acknowledged that students with learning disabilities do not suffer from lack of physical education. Youth with comorbid Learning Disability (LD)/Attention Deficit Hyperactivity Disorder (ADHD) were significantly more likely than peers without Learning Disability (LD/Attention Deficit Hyperactivity Disorder (ADHD) to be obese; the same group were significantly less likely to meet recommended levels of physical activity than the youth with learning disability only (Cook, Li, & Heinrich, 2015). The unpredicted results were confirmed when majority of teachers except three believed their learning-disabled students were engaged at the same amount of physical education as non-disabled peers. The initial literature review does not support consistency. During a 4-year period, 32 obese school-aged children were hospitalized and 26 were included in a study, over one half (57.7%) suffered from comorbid Attention Deficit Hyperactivity Disorder (ADHD) (Agranat-Meged, Deitcher, Goldzweig, Leibenson, Stein, & Galili-Weisstub, 2005). The lack of physical activity for children with learning disabilities is well documented however the teachers' account at this section contradicts with previous finding.

Factors related to lack of physical education. The three-teacher offered their expertise on factors associated with lack of physical education for learning disabled. To identify lack of physical education wait time, self-assessment on lack of needs, and mood swings were three reasons noted. Students attain to lose time if they have to wait in line or activities which negatively influence the participation. Studies confirm that sometimes children with learning disabilities can concentrate and perform well, while other times they cannot and fail to pay attention to details or having difficulty waiting in line (Public Broadcasting Service, 2002; Morin, 2017).

The ability to make effective choices and decisions is one of the most important competencies students, including those with learning disabilities can acquire. The skills of self-assessment on needs is required to be successful in life after high school. A study supports promoting student self-determination provides an excellent framework within which to teach students how to make effective choices and decisions (Hoffman, 2003). Therefore the art of decision making needs to be part of physical education programs. This will assist the students to self-assess when the behavior is not up to par.

Many students with learning disabilities show aggressive behavior, but the extent of the problem and its associated factors and effects are unclear (Tyrer, McGrother, Thorp, Donaldson, Bhaumik, Watson, & Hollin, 2006). The researchers of the study invite for further investigation of the relationship between physical aggression, frustration and mood swings in people with learning disabilities. Sleep and behavioral difficulties are common in children with developmental disabilities (Chu & Richdale, 2009) which can cause the mood swings.

In this last section teachers offer details on suggestions and experiences in helping students with learning disabilities to improve attitude in order to increase physical activity in physical education class. This portion of research is designed for current and future practices. The demand to prepare increased numbers of qualified teachers for urban schools continues to represent a major challenge nationwide (Ilmer, Elliott, Snyder, Nahan, & Colombo, 2005). The education faculty at this urban research site proposed their suggestions and experiences in confidence that other educators teaching the similar population would advance their teaching. The teaching strategies produce multiple benefits, such as clear increases in understanding and academic success as well as decreases in prejudicial attitudes (Smith, & Associates (1997) in addition suggestions for change were much appreciated (Newcombe, 2011).

Suggestions. The data revealed that the education faculty has dissimilar opinions on how to help students with learning disabilities in improving attitude in order to increase physical activity in physical education class. The suggested discerptions were divided into three sections of teachers, students, and parents which were explained previously. Afterwards the compulsory implications were alienated in two sections of physical and nonphysical units for better support. Teachers acknowledged the importance of both areas, but did not make any concrete suggestions.

All teachers suggested attitude improvements for further physical activity in physical education class made by education staff members could be related to a broader domain. Since each of the suggestions were examined by teachers, this has advanced credibility to the suggestions with respected connection to existing research. It should be noted that all suggestions made relate directly to the areas of increasing physical activity in physical education class.

At the nonphysical domain, supported by research teachers suggested that involvement, work with individual students, assistance from teachers' aides and paraprofessionals, maintaining the students on task, motivation, and encouragement (Causton-Theoharis & Malmgren, 2005; Hammel & Hourigan, 2011; Brunvand & Byrd, 2011; Butt & Lowe, 2012; Wery & Thomson, 2013). In addition it was suggested to promote class management along with increase the positive behaviors of students with disabilities (Disabled World, 2013). Aligned with research in addition teachers proposed giving praises, positive feedback, use of no passive words, consideration for boundaries, distinguishing limits, nurture but follow the established rules (Clough & Strycharczyk, 2012; Ziviani, Poulsen, & Cuskelly, 2012; Scarlett, 2015; Sousa, 2016) were used as practical suggestions. Finally, friendships with peers are important for students to develop a sense of belonging and improve overall well-being (Carter, Asmus & Moss, 2013) therefore it is imperative that student feel they are part of the class.

At the physical level teachers recommended to place efforts on coordination, differentiate instruction on absorbing games, creating enjoyable activities for motivation, and modifying rules and movements (Sheehan & Katz, 2012; Dowling, McConkey, & Hassan, 2014; Durkin, Boyle, Hunter, & Conti-Ramsden, 2015). In connection to contemporary research a teacher disclosed that some of the learning disable children are better athletes (Korbel, Lucia, Wenzel, & Anderson, 2011) hence these students should always attempt to participate to the best of their abilities. Research suggests that those with disabilities, who tend to have more health-related complications than their non-disabled peers exercise becomes very important to their health (Hinkson, 2013). As a result, a teacher recommended that students should approach the gymnasium on their lunchtime or when it is available for extra activities. A statement to design activities and utilize the space in a manner that maximizes participation (Rimmer, & Marques, 2012) was made appropriately with respective research.

Reports have transpired to show differences in the impact of structured and unstructured activities and assess parental involvement in the activity participation of children with disabilities (Brooks, 2013). This attentiveness, according to a teacher should extend to parents or caregivers to involve their children in other activities such as YMCA's and community athletics programs (Geidne & Jerlinder, 2016).

Experiences. With an average 19.1 years of experience participants communicated on how to help students with learning disabilities to improve attitude in order to increase physical activity in physical education class. Some suggested strategies which were mentioned at previous section such as, individuality, encouragement, and positive feedback were cited at experience section as well. Additionally, educators expressed tolerance, patience, forming a relationship, and provide responsibilities (El Ansari, 2011; Mărgăriţoiu, 2015) supported by research.

A faculty member suggested that based on the experience when providing students with learning disabilities many positive reinforcements, such students depart with confident experiences and look forward to the next day in the gymnasium. This lends credibility to the teacher that in fact, one way to increase physical activity is positive reinforcement (Fisher, Piazza, & Roane, 2011).

Exposure beyond traditional sports (Harada, Siperstein, Parker, & Lenox, 2011), assisting with struggled students (Grenier, 2011), and usage of music (Cousik, 2011) were additional experiences added which interpret the relationship of teachers' experiences to research.

Summary

The purpose of this qualitative case study was to understand the perceptions of physical education teachers and their experiences with learning disabled students in their classes. More specifically, this research filled the gap in the literature about attitudes that learning-disabled students have about physical education in school. Using teachers' perceptions, this study was designed to inform future practice related to teaching of physical education to students with learning disabilities. Ten certified physical education teachers assigned to PreK-12 physical education classes teaching self-contained and inclusion physical education classes participated in this qualitative case study once Institutional Review Board (IRB) approved the research. Faculty members who participated in this study responded to interview questions to answer two research questions:

Q 1. What are physical education teachers' perceptions and experiences in working with learning disabled students in their classes with respect to enjoyment and usefulness attitude components?

Q 2. How would physical education teachers describe the attitudes and behaviors of learning disabled students in their classrooms?

The theoretical framework was facilitated by analysis and organization of qualitative interview data collection. The study was organized and addressed the following related components: (a) the affective component of attitude (enjoyment), (b) the cognitive component of attitude (perceived usefulness), (c) the attitudes and behaviors of learning disabled, and (d) suggested strategies and experience of teachers:

(a)   The affective component of attitude (enjoyment), the research confirmed that children with learning disabilities exhibit positive attitudes toward physical education once enjoying the activities even though structured activities are implemented. No broad differences were noted in enjoyment of physical education between students with or without disabilities. (b) The cognitive component of attitude (perceived usefulness), the research confirmed that majority of teachers found physical education activities useful. Analysis reveals support for minimal differences in structural levels of perceived usefulness toward physical education as well as between students with or without disabilities. (c) The attitudes and behaviors of learning disabled, research confirmed that teachers believed in co-educational activities, inclusion setting and minimal lack of physical education for disabled learners. (d) Suggested strategies and experience of teachers, the maximum prevalent suggestions trusted by education staff members for improving the attitude were encouragement and positive attribution.

Chapter 5

Implications, Recommendations, and Conclusions

The problem addressed by this study was that there is limited research on how teachers perceive and assist students to participate in physical education (Eklund & Tenenbaum, 2014). Attitudes can influence whether a student will regularly engage in and continue to participate in physical education and activities (Subramaniam & Silverman et al., 2007). The factors associated with the perceptions that students with disabilities have a negative attitude toward physical education and resulting decrease in physical activity are not fully understood by teachers (Mercier, Phillip, & Silverman et al., 2016). To better understand why students are not participating in physical education, teachers' perceptions and suggested strategies for assisting children with learning disabilities was assessed. Teachers' perspectives and suggested strategies in assisting students with learning disabilities in order to increase physical activity are needed to guide physical educators to teach their students (Cheon, Reeve, & Moon, 2012; Harwell,& Jackson, 2014).

The purpose of this qualitative case study was to understand the perceptions of physical education teachers and their experiences with learning disabled students in their classes. More specifically, this research filled the gap in the literature about attitudes that learning-disabled students have about physical education in school. Using teachers' perceptions, this study was designed to inform future practice related to teaching of physical education to students with learning disabilities. Teachers' perceptions of these students' attitudes toward participation in physical education was assessed through semi-structured interviews of teachers.

The population consisted of 10 physical education teachers assigned to Pre-Kindergarten-12 physical education classes in a district in Northeast of the United States participated in this study. Semi-structured interviews contained of 10 questions guided the researcher in answering two research questions. The ten formal interview questions were intended to elicit elaborations on the perceptions and experiences in working with learning disabled students in addition to the attitudes and behaviors of learning disabled students in physical education setting constructed empirically evaluated during this quantitative study (Teddlie & Tashakkori et al., 2009).

This study had three limitations. First limitation was that the interviews were performed over a brief restricted time therefore, it was not a longitudinal study extended over a long period. This potentially minimized the findings not to show any trends over an extended period of time. The second limitation was the district and number of teachers' participants. This study occurred within ten physical education content area teachers in one school district in Northeast of the United States. This smaller sample size optimistically would result in use of provided data. The final limitation was with the data collection. The teacher-participant interview questions were carefully designed to avoid use of leading questions. The questions were field-tested by three experts and suggested changes were implemented. Nevertheless, provided questions and conducted face-to-face interviews might put limitations on the study due to possible bias which might influenced the interview interactions and participant responses. Nonetheless the researcher's personal considerations were separated from the session to the best of ability.

Considerations were given to the potential human subjects' implications therefore seeking approval from Northcentral University Institutional Review Board (IRB), prior to the commencement of any data collection, was adhered for the ethical principles. All procedures for the code of ethics at Northcentral University (NCU) were followed and pursued required guidelines at the Institutional Review Board (IRB). No financial or supervisory conflicts of interest existed between the teachers and researcher. In addition, informed consent forms were obtained from all participants. Confidentiality of the participants and their responses were considered throughout the study. All data was de-identified when presented in this study.

The reminder of this final chapter provides an overview of the implications, recommendations, and the conclusion of the study with respect to existing literature and its potential application. This document is a logical contribution to physical education of students with learning disabilities.

Implications

Researchers have examined the attitudes of students with disabilities in school based physical education programs over the past 30 years. The approached topic is largely from the perspectives of the general physical education teacher or from the perspectives of non-disabled students (Smith & Thomas, 2006; Coates & Vickerman, 2008). Fundamentally research studies have investigated attitudes a single framed component. This study not only organized around a two-component attitude theory (Subramaniam & Silverman et al., 2007) in perception and experiences of working with learning disabled but rather strived for teachers to describe the attitudes and behaviors of leaning disabled and suggest strategies to improve and increase physical activity during physical education. The research questions that guided this study are presented with implications of the findings.

Research Question 1. What are physical education teachers' perceptions and experiences in working with learning disabled students in their classes with respect to enjoyment and usefulness attitude components?

The first research question was addressed through individual interview sessions with physical education teachers of Pre-Kindergarten to 12. Data was analyzed using manual coding analysis process. Participants identified the physical education class influenced by enjoyment and usefulness of physical education. This section will explain on enjoyment first and then proceed to usefulness.

Enjoyment. Positive relationship between enjoyment of physical education for both students with/without disabilities and structured instructions have remained to be a strong predictor of increased student participation and attitudes in school (Yli-Piipari, Watt, Jaakkola, Liukkonen, & Nurmi, 2009). Previous related research studies have confirmed the importance of enjoyment in physical education class on student attitudes toward participation and engagement in physical education related activities (Bryan & Solmon, 2012).

As indicated previously, the present study's data agrees with special education literature regarding modifications of movements in terms of enjoyment in physical education (Winnick & Porretta el at., 2016). Consistent with current study results teachers have engaged students in activities by encouragements and motivations. This is supported by evidence supporting that modification of lessons and encouragement of students result in enjoyment (Gråstén, Jaakkola, Liukkonen, Watt, & Yli-Piipari, 2012).

Drawn from skill level, effective practices are ensured by physical education teachers.

Students with minimum developed motor abilities are provided with opportunities to engage in activities that suit their skills' levels by teachers' selected activities. This factor increases positive attitudes toward physical education and enhance participation. This section confirmed that physical education teachers produce an essential and critical role in ensuring that all students are motivated and engaged in classroom activities.

Usefulness. Prior research attempts have shown that students are significantly more likely to engage in physical education when activities are meaningful, interesting, and hold personal relevance (Haerens, D., Cardon, & De Bourdeaudhuij, 2011; Haerens, Aelterman, Van den Berghe, De Meyer, Soenens, & Vansteenkiste, 2013; Van den Berghe, Vansteenkiste, Cardon, Kirk, D., & Haerens, 2014). Majority of teachers believed that their lessons were useful due to assistance with coordination, personal development, socialization and activities out of school settings. Structured lessons were implemented for both children with/without disabilities.

In conclusion of research question 1 at the implication level it is necessary to emphasize that this study was structured around an examination of attitude through two component directions and did not emphasis exclusively on one single theoretical explanation for student attitude. The teachers' structured lessons served as the strongest theme at the point of factors influencing enjoyment and perceived usefulness of participants. A positive finding from research question # 1 is that the factor identified by participants is given attention to students' abilities to increase participation in physical education activities.

Research Question 2. How would physical education teachers describe the attitudes and behaviors of learning disabled students in their classrooms?

Participants at this section specifically concentrated on attitudes concerning inclusion vs self-contained, co-education vs single sex education, lack of physical activity in physical education class, factors related to lack of physical education, suggestions and experiences.

Inclusion vs self-contained. The critical components of inclusion vs. self-contained physical education instructions for students with disabilities was questioned. Teachers responded that in order to increase positive attitude and behavior of students with learning disabilities in physical education participation, self-contained physical education environment possibly is necessary however it does not despicable to more restricted environment. In the study the differences were noted with almost teachers divided in half responding to the question. Literature regarding effective practices for inclusion and self-contained with a focus on critical components of successful trends of both settings have existed (Kim, 2011; Odom, Buysse, & Soukakou, 2011; Roth, Zittel, Pyfer, & Auxter, 2016). Teachers' concentration remained on effectively engaging students with disabilities in physical education classes. This view provides evidence that students should have access to both settings in order to increase attitude and progress at school (Lohman, 2011).

Co-education vs single sex education. Co-physical education continues to be a topic of debate among educators. This question was uniformly answered. All teachers provided negatively overviewed of single sex education except in eight grade swimming lessons where attitude became problematic. Based on the gathered data educators trust that with the gender integration of physical education classes, the issue of inequity for boys and girls would be diminished (Mahony, 2012). Aside from the equity view, enjoyment of physical education is declined among girls but remained constant among boys. Lower perceived athletic competence is associated with low enjoyment of physical education, among girls, with declining enjoyment (Cairney, Kwan, Velduizen, Hay, Bray, & Faught, 2012). Nevertheless, data from this study confirms no decline of enjoyment for females was present.

Lack of physical activity in physical education class. Supporting evidence provisioned that children with disability engage in less physical activity compared to their typically developing peers (Frey & Stanish, 2008; Woodmansee, Hahne, Imms, & Shields, 2016). Almost every recent research confirms lack of physical activity in physical education class for disabled students due to attitude. Yet this study confirms different results from those presented previously. Greater number of participants considered no lack of physical activity in physical education for children with disabilities. This conflicting result with the current research settles for attitude divergent.

Factors related to lack of physical education. The obstacles in regards to participation in physical activity have been studied comprehensively and include a lack of knowledge and skills, the child's preferences, fear, parental behavior, negative attitudes to disability, inadequate facilities, lack of transport, lack of programmers and staff capacity, and cost (Shields, Synnot, & Barr, 2012). Since majority of physical education teachers did not embrace lack of physical education for students with disabilities few restricted new knowledge was applied to this section. Factors such as outside influences, wait time, and lack of motivation were noted. Influences explaining on differences of opinions were not explored as a part of this study.

Suggestions and experiences. Offering suggestions and experiences, teachers shared their expertise for current and future professionals. There was no specific finding in this study rather rich attributions on how current and future professionals can effectively contribute to learning environment of leaning disabled in physical education classes. Teacher experience has long been a central pillar of teacher workforce policies in U.S. school systems (Rice, 2013). The data collected in this section projected on attitude and behavior of students. It can be presumed that these identified finding can now be used to develop physical education effective practices and interventions.

Recommendations

This section contains the recommendations based on the results from this study. The findings of this study present an opportunity to improve practices at the specific district where the study was conducted and moreover provide a foundation for other potential research attempts. Investigation of participants' insights and experiences assisted to define factors that influence attitudes. Recommendations for educators in the field of physical education and for future research are offered in the following paragraphs.

Recommendations for the field

During this study, education staff members provided comprehensive responses regarding essential areas in attitudes of students with learning disabilities during physical activity in physical education class. This study was directed toward the importance of the physical education teachers in addressing enjoyment and perceived usefulness during physical activity in physical education class. In understanding of this study's results, four recommendations for the field of physical education are offered.

First, it is recommended that physical educators consider interaction with students during class activities, offer encouragement and propose motivation. Students with learning disabilities often become frustrated due to feeling of incompetency in many areas of school (Weiser, 2014). The results from the data of this study showed strong correlation between motivations as point of encouragement. Integrating intrinsic motivation with behavioral interventions are leading to many academic and social/emotional improvements among K-12 students (Froiland, Oros, Smith, & Hirchert, 2012). Strategies are only beneficial when students are motivated. Studies disclosed that positive attributions regarding effort can motivate children with mild learning disabilities (Berkeley, Mastropieri, & Scruggs, 2011). For individuals with disabilities, meaningful and intrinsically motivated leisure activities foster mental health (Palisano, Chiarello, King, Novak, Stoner, & Fiss, 2012).

Second, study participants overwhelmingly supported the co-education practices. The research found similar and opposing views (Hills, 2007; Annerstedt, 2008;

Fagrell, Larsson, & Redelius, 2012) nevertheless for the purposes of this research at given setting, mixed gender does not impose any negative effects on students' attitude. Perceived physical differences and abilities between boys and girls, especially in adolescence, have traditionally formed a foundation upon constructing physical education programs. A study explored the pursuit of equal opportunity for girls in school physical education through liberal reform strategies, such as antidiscrimination legislation and coeducational initiatives (Vertinsky, 2012). Thus, schools should investigate whether their physical education programs are truly meeting the needs of both genders (Smiley, 2015). As a result teachers in this study did not pursue gender segregation, therefore it is recommended to support equal access to physical education programs at any level of Pre-Kindergarten-12 grades.

Further, physical educators must consider lessons which are intensely structured (Roth et al., 2016). Grounded in this study unstructured environment does not guarantee enjoyment or usefulness in physical education. Faculties should be mindful of students with disabilities and continue structured lessons plans as it is operating efficiently. A physical education class demands rigidity structure, providing students with opportunities for social interactions will likely originate benefits for both physical education and academic content area classes (Wentzel, 2009; Richards & Templin, 2011). It is recommended that physical education teachers respect socialization among students during physical education while maintaining course objectives.

Fourth, with respect to this research it is recommended that teachers continue to the best of instructional abilities to educate all students in inclusion or self-contained gymnasiums. Inclusion remains as effective practices for all students (McLeskey, Rosenberg, & Westling, 2012). For many physical educators, the spectrum of teaching styles serves as a tool box for meeting the different needs of students and goals in physical education (Sanchez, Byra, Wallhead, 2012). Therefore, Modification at some levels may become necessary as recommended by few teachers however teachers should remain and continue to implement the district's approved curriculum.

As a side note at training level as recommended by two teachers policy makers optimistically should adhere to implementation of professional development sessions for physical education teachers on students with learning disabilities. Colleges and universities should be mandated to offer additional courses in respect to children with disabilities.

Recommendation for future research

There is a deficiency of research with respect to the attitudes of students toward physical education during physical activity and as a result research in this area needs to continue. Taking to consideration of present study results two recommendations are presented for future research.

First, as most studies on children with disabilities are conducted on teachers, parents and children without disability it is recommended that additional research consider children with disability as sample size. Change in policy and practice directly affecting students is often based on adult perspectives rather than student perspectives (Cook-Sather, 2011). Studies examining the attitudes of students with disabilities in school-based physical education programs have frequently approached the topic from the perspectives of the general physical education teacher (Coates & Vickerman, 2013). It is recommended that information directly be collected from students.

Second, inconsistent with the finding of this research study whether there is a lack of physical education for students with disabilities need to be explore further. Physical educators may possibly encounter the unique needs of students with learning disabilities so that disabilities do not negatively affect participation in physical education as this research indicated. Yet, students with intellectual disabilities, including those in the profound range of disability, suffer up to 50% more health-related issues than individuals without disabilities (Townsend, 2011). Conflicting research with current one indicate that individuals with disabilities are at increased risk for complications associated with a sedentary lifestyle than individuals without disabilities (Mansell & Beadle-Brown, J. 2012). Extensive research with a larger sample is necessary to add to the body of knowledge.

Conclusion

The current views of educators provided a foundation for reflecting upon related findings from data collected by participants. All of which that supports structured physical education program to exhibit positive attitudes toward physical education. Besides structured lessons, teachers included that all children are involved in curriculum. This method exemplifies the "least-restrictive environment" required for a non-ambulatory students. Encouraging growth at every level is direct impact of education.

Quantitative results from this study revealed that attitude of students with and without disabilities largely remain the same at enjoyment and useful levels. The degree of difference is minimal and more similarities were found between students with and without disabilities than differences in this study. After all students exhibit positive attitudes toward physical education at enjoyment and useful levels. Qualitative data provided teachers' perception into the factors that produced role of students with learning disabilities participating actively in physical education. This notion relates to presumed assumption that students with learning disabilities engage in significantly less physical activity than their nondisabled peers in physical education class (Shields et al., 2009; Zhang et al., 2009; U.S. Government Accountability Office et al., 2011; Lotan et al., 2015) which is not supported by the finding of this research. With such awareness, findings suggest that it is the success of this particular physical education program at respected district.

The benefits of active participation in physical education and activities are extensively documented in the study. Seven themes were identified as influential factors in attitude dimensions, extracted from the interview questions and explained deeply in previous chapters: (a) enjoyment, (b) usefulness, (c) inclusion, (d) co-education, (e) limited lack of physical education, (f) factors in lack of physical education, and (g) suggestions and experiences. Education staff have meaningful jurisdiction throughout all these factors influencing students' attitudes toward physical education.

Considerations to recognized issues influencing the attitudes of students with learning disabilities toward physical education positively will result in progressive effects. Lou Holtz, the former American football player, coach, and analyst once said, "Ability is what you're capable of doing. Motivation determines what you do. Attitude determines how well you do it". The ability of teachers is to motive and encourage students to rise above and beyond with positive attitude.

This study may initiate future studies in the field however at a different educational settings, geographical regions or with different age groups and education staff members nevertheless it will serve purposely of educating the next generation of healthy adults.

References

Abdi, E. (2015). 'Theoretical Literature Review on Lack of Cardiorespiratory Fitness and Its Effects on Children'. *World Academy of Science, Engineering and Technology, International Science Index* 103, 9(7).

Abdi, E., & Juniu, S. (2015). Interdisciplinary Integrated Physical Education Program Using a Philosophical Approach. *Social, Behavioral, Educational, Economic and Management Engineering, 8*(8), 2736-2742.

Adapted physical education standards. (2008). What is adapted physical education. Retrieved from http://www.apens.org/whatisape.html

Agranat-Meged, A. N., Deitcher, C., Goldzweig, G., Leibenson, L., Stein, M., & Galili-Weisstub, E. (2005). Childhood obesity and attention deficit/ hyperactivity disorder: a newly described comorbidity in obese hospitalized children. *International Journal of Eating Disorders, 37*(4), 357-359.

Ajzen, I. (2001). Nature and operation of attitudes. *Annual review of psychology, 52*(1), 27-58.

Allen, M. P. (2015). The Promotion of Self-Determination: A Survey of General and Special Educators.

Allport, G. W. (1935). Attitudes.

American Heart Association. (2008). *Policy Position Statement on Physical Education in Schools.* Dallas, TX: http://www.heart.org/idc/groups/heart- public/@wcm/@ adv/documents/downloadable/ucm_301654.pdf.

American Heart Association. (2015). NFL Play 60 challenge. Retrieved from http:// www.heart.org/HEARTORG/Educator/FortheClassroom/Play60Challenge/ PLAY- 60-Challenge

American Speech-Language-Hearing Association. (2014). Understanding the language of special education. Retrieved from http://www.charterarts.org/wp-content/uploads/2014/09/Understanding-the-Language-of-Special-Ed.pdf

Anastasiou, D., & Kauffman, J. M. (2013). The social model of disability: Dichotomy between impairment and disability. *Journal of Medicine and Philosophy, 38*(4), 441-459.

Annerstedt, C. (2008). Physical education in Scandinavia with a focus on Sweden: a comparative perspective. *Physical Education and Sport Pedagogy, 13*(4), 303-318.

Anxiety Disorders Association of America. (2010). *Understanding anxiety.* Retrieved from: http://www.adaa.org/understanding-anxiety

Arabacı, R. (2009). Attitudes toward physical education and class preferences of Turkish secondary and high school students. *İlköğretim Online, 8*(1).

Ardoy, D. N., Fernández-Rodríguez, J. M., Jiménez-Pavón, D., Castillo, R., Ruiz, J. R., & Ortega, F. B. (2014). A Physical Education trial improves adolescents' cognitive performance and academic achievement: the EDUFIT study. *Scandinavian journal of medicine & science in sports, 24*(1), e52-e61.

ATTENTION-DEFICIT, S. O. (2011). ADHD: clinical practice guideline for the diagnosis, evaluation, and treatment of attention-deficit/hyperactivity disorder in children and adolescents. *Pediatrics*, peds-2011.

Bagozzi, R. P., & Burnkrant, R. E. (1985). Attitude organization and the attitude behavior relationship: A reply to Dillon and Kumar. Journal of Personality and Social Psychology, 49(1), 47-57. doi: 10.1037/0022-3514.49.1.47

Bailey, R., Wellard, I., & Dismore, H. (2014). Girls' participation in physical activities and sports: Benefits, patterns, influences and ways forward; 2004.

Ballard, K. (2016). Children and disability: Special or included. *Waikato Journal of Education, 10*(1).

Bandini, L., Danielson, M., Esposito, L. E., Foley, J. T., Fox, M. H., Frey, G. C., & Rodgers, A. B. (2015). Obesity in children with developmental and/or physical disabilities. *Disability and health journal, 8*(3), 309-316.

Barr-Anderson, D. J., Neumark-Sztainer, D., Lytle, L., Schmitz, K. H., Ward, D. S., Conway, T. L., & Pate, R. R. (2008). But I like PE: Factors associated with enjoyment of physical education class in middle school girls. *Research quarterly for exercise and sport, 79*(1), 18-27.

Barr, M., & Shields, N. (2011). Identifying the barriers and facilitators to participation in physical activity for children with Down syndrome. *Journal of Intellectual Disability Research, 55*(11), 1020-1033.

Barroso, C. S., Kelder, S. H., Springer, A. E., Smith, C. L., Ranjit, N., Ledingham, C., & Hoelscher, D. M. (2009). Senate Bill 42: implementation and impact on physical activity in middle schools. *Journal of Adolescent Health, 45*(3), S82-S90.

Bartlo, P., & Klein, P. J. (2011). Physical activity benefits and needs in adults with intellectual disabilities: Systematic review of the literature. *American Journal on Intellectual and Developmental Disabilities, 116*(3), 220-232.

Basterfield, L., Adamson, A. J., Frary, J. K., Parkinson, K. N., Pearce, M. S., & Reilly, J. J. (2011). Longitudinal study of physical activity and sedentary behavior in children. *Pediatrics, 127*(1), e24-e30.

Bedell, G., Coster, W., Law, M., Liljenquist, K., Kao, Y. C., Teplicky, R., & Khetani, M. A. (2013). Community participation, supports, and barriers of school-age children with and without disabilities. *Archives of Physical Medicine and Rehabilitation, 94*(2), 315-323.

Belton, S., O'Brien, W., Meegan, S., Woods, C., & Issartel, J. (2014). Youth-Physical Activity Towards Health: evidence and background to the development of the Y-PATH physical activity intervention for adolescents. *BMC Public Health, 14*(1), 1.

Bennie, A., Peralta, L., Gibbons, S., Lubans, D., & Rosenkranz, R. (2016). Physical education teachers' perceptions about the effectiveness and acceptability of strategies used to increase relevance and choice for students in physical education classes. *Asia-Pacific Journal of Teacher Education*, 1-18.

Berger, N. A., Müller, A., Brähler, E., Philipsen, A., & de Zwaan, M. (2014). Association of symptoms of attention-deficit/hyperactivity disorder with symptoms of excessive exercising in an adult general population sample. *BMC psychiatry, 14*(1), 1.

Berkeley, S., Mastropieri, M. A., & Scruggs, T. E. (2011). Reading comprehension strategy instruction and attribution retraining for secondary students with learning and other mild disabilities. *Journal of Learning Disabilities, 44*(1), 18-32.

Bernstein, E., Phillips, S. R., & Silverman, S. (2011). Attitudes and perceptions of middle school students toward competitive activities in physical education. *Journal of teaching in physical education, 30*(1), 69-83.

Besharat Pour, M., Bergström, A., Bottai, M., Kull, I., Wickman, M., Håkansson, N., & Moradi, T. (2014). Effect of parental migration background on childhood nutrition, physical activity, and body mass index. *Journal of obesity, 2014*.

Beyer, C. J., & Davis, E. A. (2012). Learning to critique and adapt science curriculum materials: Examining the development of preservice elementary teachers' pedagogical content knowledge. *Science Education, 96*(1), 130-157.

Beyer, R., Flores, M. M., & Vargas-Tonsing, T. M. (2008). Coaches' attitudes towards youth sport participants with attention deficit hyperactivity disorder. *International Journal of Sports Science & Coaching, 3*(4), 555-563.

Bibik, J. M., Goodwin, S. C., & Orsega-Smith, E. M. (2007). High school students' attitudes toward physical education in Delaware. *Physical Educator, 64*(4), 192.

Bicard, D. F. (2000). Using classroom rules to construct behavior. Middle School Journal, 31 (5), 37–45.

Biggs, J. B. (2011). *Teaching for quality learning at university: What the student does.* McGraw-Hill Education (UK).

Bingham, D. D., Boddy, L. M., Ridgers, N. D., & Stratton, G. (2015). The Physical Activity Levels and Play Behaviours of Children with Special Needs: An Exploratory Cross- sectional Study. *Archives of Exercise in Health and Disease, 5*(1-2), 359-365.

Biro, F. M., & Wien, M. (2010). Childhood obesity and adult morbidities. *The American journal of clinical nutrition, 91*(5), 1499S-1505S.

Blake, C. D. (2012). *Single-sex education versus coeducation in north Georgia public middle schools*

Block, M. E., & Obrusnikova, I. (2007). Inclusion in physical education: A review of the literature from 1995-2005. *Adapted Physical Activity Quarterly, 24*(2), 103.

Bloomberg, L. D., & Volpe, M. (2015). *Completing your qualitative dissertation: A road map from beginning to end.* Sage Publications.

Blum, L. M. (2015). *Raising generation Rx: Mothering kids with invisible disabilities in an age of inequality.* NYU Press.

Bouchard, C., Blair, S. N., & Haskell, W. (2012). *Physical activity and health.* Human Kinetics.

Boyle, C., Topping, K., Jindal-Snape, D., & Norwich, B. (2012). The importance of peer-support for teaching staff when including children with special educational needs. *School Psychology International, 33*(2), 167-184.

Brabo, H. (2013). Class size matters: impact of class size on differentiating instruction in high school physical education. Dominican University. Retrieved from http://scholar.dominican.edu/cgi/viewcontent.

Braun, R., & Braun, B. (2015). Managing the Challenges of Hidden Disabilities in Youth Sport: A Look at SLD, ADHD, and ASD through the Sport Psychology Lens. *Journal of Sport Psychology in Action, 6*(1), 28-43.

Bridge, C. (2014). Motivational Interviewing and Group Work. *Motivational Interviewing Children and Young People‖: Issues and Further Applications*, 61.

Brinkmann, S. (2014). *Interview* (pp. 1008-1010). Springer New York.

Brooks, B. A. (2013). Extracurricular activities and the development of social skills in children with intellectual and learning disabilities.

Brown, H. E., Pearson, N., Braithwaite, R. E., Brown, W. J., & Biddle, S. J. (2013). Physical activity interventions and depression in children and adolescents. *Sports medicine, 43*(3), 195-206.

Brunet, J., Sabiston, C. M., O'Loughlin, J., Mathieu, M. E., Tremblay, A., Barnett, T. A., & Lambert, M. (2014). Perceived parental social support and moderate-to-vigorous physical activity in children at risk of obesity. *Research quarterly for exercise and sport, 85*(2), 198-207.

Brunvand, S., & Byrd, S. (2011). Using Voice: Thread to promote learning engagement and success for all students. *Teaching Exceptional Children, 43*(4), 28-37.

Bryan, C. L., & Solmon, M. A. (2012). Student motivation in physical education and engagement in physical activity. *Journal of sport behavior, 35*(3), 267.

Buchanan, J., Prescott, A., Schuck, S., Aubusson, P., Burke, P., & Louviere, J. (2013). Teacher retention and attrition: Views of early career teachers. *Australian Journal of Teacher Education, 38*(3), 8.

Burrows, R., Correa, P., & Ibaceta, C. (2014). Scheduled physical activity is associated with better academic performance in Chilean school-age children. *J Phys Act Health.*

Butt, R., & Lowe, K. (2012). Teaching assistants and class teachers: Differing perceptions, role confusion and the benefits of skills-based training. *International Journal of Inclusive Education, 16*(2), 207-219.

Cairney, J., Kwan, M. Y., Velduizen, S., Hay, J., Bray, S. R., & Faught, B. E. (2012). Gender, perceived competence and the enjoyment of physical education in children: a longitudinal examination. *International Journal of Behavioral Nutrition and Physical Activity, 9*(1), 26.

California Department of Education. (2013). *Physical education FAQs.* Retrieved from http://www.cde.ca.gov/pd/ca/pe/physeducfaqs.asp

Campos, M. J., Ferreira, J. P., & Block, M. E. (2015). Exploring teachers' voices about inclusion in physical education: a qualitative analysis with young elementary and middle school teachers 1. *innovative teaching, 4*(1), Article-5.

Carlson, S. A., Fulton, J. E., Lee, S. M., Foley, J. T., Heitzler, C., & Huhman, M. (2010). Influence of limit-setting and participation in physical activity on youth screen time. *Pediatrics, 126*(1), e89-e96.

Carlson, S. A., Fulton, J. E., Lee, S. M., Maynard, L. M., Brown, D. R., Kohl III, H. W., & Dietz, W. H. (2008). Physical education and academic achievement in elementary school: data from the early childhood longitudinal study. *American journal of public health, 98*(4), 721-727.

Carter, E. W., Asmus, J., & Moss, C. K. (2013). Fostering friendships: Supporting relationships among youth with and without developmental disabilities. *The Prevention Researcher, 20*(2), 14-18.

Causton-Theoharis, J. N., & Malmgren, K. W. (2005). Increasing peer interactions for students with severe disabilities via paraprofessional training. *Exceptional children, 71*(4), 431- 444.

Cawley, J., Frisvold, D., & Meyerhoefer, C. (2013). The impact of physical education on obesity among elementary school children. *Journal of Health Economics, 32*(4), 743-755.

Center for Disease Control and Prevention. (2010). The Association Between School-Based Physical Activity, Including Physical Education, and Academic Performance. Atlanta, GA: U.S. Department of Health and Human Services.

Center for Disease Control and Prevention. (2011). National diabetes fact sheet: national estimates and general information on diabetes and prediabetes in the United States, Atlanta, GA: U.S. Department of Health and Human Services.

Centers for Disease Control. (2013). Make a difference at your school-United States 2013 report.

Center for Disease Control and Prevention. (2013). Youth Risk Behavior Surveillance—United States, 2013. *MMWR* 2014;63(SS-4).

Centers for Disease Control and Prevention, (2015). Defining childhood obesity. Retrieved from https://www.cdc.gov/obesity/childhood/defining.html

Center for Parent Information and Resources. (2016). Part B of IDEA: services for school-aged children. Retrieved from http://www.parentcenterhub.org/repository/partb/

Cheon, S. H., Reeve, J., & Moon, I. S. (2012). Experimentally based, longitudinally designed, teacher-focused intervention to help physical education teachers be more autonomy supportive toward their students. *Journal of Sport & Exercise Psychology, 34*(3), 365- 396.

Children's Hospital of Philadelphia. 2016. *Inclusion vs. self-contained education for children with ASD diagnoses.* Retrieved from https://www.carautismroadmap.org/inclusion-vs- self-contained-education-for-children-with-asd-diagnoses/

Children with Special Healthcare Needs in Context: a portrait of the states and the nation. (2007). Retrieved from http://mchb.hrsa.gov/nsch/07cshcn/

Chiviacowsky, S., Wulf, G., & Avila, L. T. G. (2013). An external focus of attention enhances motor learning in children with intellectual disabilities. *Journal of Intellectual Disability Research*, *57*(7), 627-634.

Chomitz, V. R., Slining, M. M., McGowan, R. J., Mitchell, S. E., Dawson, G. F., & Hacker, K. A. (2009). Is there a relationship between physical fitness and academic achievement? Positive results from public school children in the northeastern United States. *Journal of School Health*, *79*(1), 30-37.

Chow, B. C., McKenzie, T. L., & Louie, L. (2015). Children's physical activity and associated variables during preschool physical education. *Advances in Physical Education*, *5*(01), 39.

Chu, J., & Richdale, A. L. (2009). Sleep quality and psychological wellbeing in mothers of children with developmental disabilities. *Research in developmental disabilities*, *30*(6), 1512-1522.

Chute, E. (2010). Report: Too many students placed in special education: City doing better reducing numbers. *McClatchy-Tribune Business News*. Washington. Retrieved from http://proquest.umi.com.proxy1. ncu.edu/pqdweb

Clapham, E. D., & Lamont, L. S. (2015). Catching Waves for Health: Exploring the Benefits of Surfing. In *research quarterly for exercise and sport* (vol. 86, pp. a12-a12).

Clark, V. P., & Creswell, J. W. (2011). Designing and conducting mixed methods research.

Clough, P., & Strycharczyk, D. (2012). *Developing mental toughness: improving performance, wellbeing and positive behaviour in others*. Kogan Page Publishers.

Coates, J., & Vickerman, P. (2008). Let the children have their say: children with special educational needs and their experiences of physical education—a review. *Support for Learning*, *23*(4), 168-175.

Coates, J., & Vickerman, P. (2013). A review of methodological strategies for consulting children with special educational needs in physical education. *European Journal of Special Needs Education*, *28*(3), 333-347.

Cobigo, V., & Stuart, H. (2010). Social inclusion and mental health. *Current Opinion in Psychiatry*, *23*(5), 453-457.

Code of Federal Regulations. (2004). Title 34, §300.8(c)(4)(ii). Retrieved form http://www.parentcenterhub.org/repository/emotionaldisturbance

Collins, R. (2012). *Attitudes of Middle School Students With Disabilities Toward Physical Education: A Mixed Methods Examination*. Northcentral University.

Combs, S., Elliott, S., & Whipple, K. (2010). Elementary Physical Education Teachers' Attitudes towards the Inclusion of Children with Special Needs: A Qualitative Investigation. *International Journal of Special Education*, *25*(1), 114-125.

Cone, T. P., & Cone, S. L. (2011). Strategies for teaching dancers of all abilities. *Journal of Physical Education, Recreation & Dance*, *82*(2), 24-31.

Conroy, P. (2012). Supporting Students with Visual Impairments in Physical Education: Needs of Physical Educators. *Insight: Research & Practice in Visual Impairment & Blindness*, *5*(1).

Conway, M. A. (2014). Introduction: Disability studies meets special education. *Review of Disability Studies: An International Journal*, *1*(3).

Cook, B. G., Li, D., & Heinrich, K. M. (2015). Obesity, physical activity, and sedentary behavior of youth with learning disabilities and ADHD. *Journal of learning disabilities*, *48*(6), 563-576.

Cook, B. G., Tankersley, M., & Landrum, T. J. (Eds.). (2013). *Evidence-based practices* (Vol. 26). Emerald Group Publishing.

Cook, R. E., Klein, M. D., & Chen, D. (2015). *Adapting early childhood curricula for children with special needs*. Pearson.

Cook-Sather, A. (2011). Layered learning: Student consultants deepening classroom and life lessons. *Educational Action Research*, *19*(1), 41-57.

Cope, D. G. (2014, January). Methods and meanings: credibility and trustworthiness of qualitative research. In *Oncology nursing forum* (Vol. 41, No. 1).

Correa-Burrows, P., Burrows, R., Ibaceta, C., Orellana, Y., & Ivanovic, D. (2014). Physically active Chilean school kids perform better in language and mathematics. *Health promotion international*, dau010.

Cortiella, C., & Horowitz, S. H. (2014). The state of learning disabilities: Facts, trends and emerging issues. *New York: National Center for Learning Disabilities*.

Cosgriff, M. (2000). Walking our talk: Adventure based learning and physical education. *New Zealand Physical Educator*, *33*(2), 89.

Cote, J., Baker, J., & Abernethy, B. (2003). From play to practice. *Expert performance in sports: Advances in research on sport expertise. United State: Human Kinetics*, 89-113.

Cothran, D. O. N. E. T. T. A., & Kulinna, P. A. M. E. L. A. (2015). Classroom management in physical education. *Handbook of classroom management*, 239-260.

Council for Children with Behavioral Disorder (2003). Council for Children with Behavior Disorders Position Brief on Overrepresentation of Ethnic Minorities in Special Education. Position brief from CCBD (over-representation). Retrieved from http://www.ccbd.net/content.cfm

Council for Exceptional Children. (2015). Behavior disorders: definitions, characteristics & related information. Retrieved from http://www.ccbd.net/about/ebddefintion

Council on Sports Medicine and Fitness & Council on School Health. (2006). Active healthy living: Prevention of childhood obesity through increased physical activity. Pediatrics, 117, 1834-1842. Retrieved from http://aappolicy.aappublications.org

Cousik, R. (2011). *A case study of four children with multiple risk factors in a music class*. Indiana University.

Craigie, A. M., Lake, A. A., Kelly, S. A., Adamson, A. J., & Mathers, J. C. (2011). Tracking of obesity-related behaviours from childhood to adulthood: a systematic review. *Maturitas, 70*(3), 266-284.

Crano, W. D., & Prislin, R. (2006). Attitudes and persuasion. *Annu. Rev. Psychol., 57*, 345-374.

Creswell, J. W. (2009). Editorial: Mapping the field of mixed methods research. *Journal of Mixed Methods Research, 3*(2), 95-108.

Creswell, J. W. (2012). *Qualitative inquiry and research design: Choosing among five approaches*. Sage.

Creswell, J. W. (2013). *Research design: Qualitative, quantitative, and mixed methods approaches*. Sage publications.

Crockett, J. B., & Kauffman, J. M. (2013). *The least restrictive environment: Its origins and interpretations in special education*. Routledge.

Cumming, R., Wilson, A., & Goswami, U. (2015). Basic auditory processing and sensitivity to prosodic structure in children with specific language impairments: a new look at a perceptual hypothesis. *Frontiers in psychology, 6*.

Daniels, S. R., Arnett, D. K., Eckel, R. H., Gidding, S. S., Hayman, L. L., & Kumanyika, S. (2005). Robinson TN, Scott BJ, Jero SSt. Williams CL. Overweight in Children and Adolescents: Pathophysiology, Consequences. *Prevention and Treatment. American Heart Association Scientific Statement. Circulation, 111*, 1999-2012.

Data Display: New Jersey. (2011). Identification of children with disabilities. Retrieved from https://www2.ed.gov/fund/data/report/idea/partbspap/2013/nj-acc-stateprofile-11-12.pdf

Davidson, T. (1896). *Aristotle and ancient educational ideals* (Vol. 1). C. Scribner's sons.

Davis, C. L., Tomporowski, P. D., McDowell, J. E., Austin, B. P., Miller, P. H., Yanasak, N. E., & Naglieri, J. A. (2011). Exercise improves executive function and achievement and alters brain activation in overweight children: a randomized, controlled trial. *Health Psychology, 30*(1), 91.

Davis, K. E. B., & Hardin, S. E. (2013). Making STEM fun: How to organize a STEM camp. *Teaching Exceptional Children, 45*(4), 60-67.

de Casterle, B. D., Gastmans, C., Bryon, E., & Denier, Y. (2012). QUAGOL: a guide for qualitative data analysis. *International journal of nursing studies, 49*(3), 360-371.

Denscombe, M. (2014). *The good research guide: for small-scale social research projects.* McGraw-Hill Education (UK).

Diament. M. (2011). Obesity more common among kids with special needs. Disability scoop.

Retrieved from http://www.disabilityscoop.com/2011/12/07/obesity-special-needs/14599/

Di Nardo, M., Kudláček, M., Tafuri, D., & Sklenaříková, J. (2014). Attitudes of preservice physical educators toward individuals with disabilities at University Parthenope of Napoli. *Acta Gymnica, 44*(4), 211-221.

Disabled World. (2013). Music therapy for people with disabilities. Retrieved from http://www.disabled-world.com/medical/rehabilitation/therapy/music.php

Dismore, H., & Bailey, R. (2010). 'It's been a bit of a rocky start': attitudes toward physical education following transition. *Physical Education and Sport Pedagogy, 15*(2), 175-191.

Dodd, L. J., Al-Nakeeb, Y., Nevill, A., & Forshaw, M. J. (2010). Lifestyle risk factors of students: a cluster analytical approach. *Preventive medicine, 51*(1), 73-77.

Donnelly, J. E., & Lambourne, K. (2011). Classroom-based physical activity, cognition, and academic achievement. *Preventive medicine, 52*, S36-S42.

Doody, C. M., & Doody, O. (2012). Health promotion for people with intellectual disability and obesity.

Doulkeridou, A., Evaggelinou, C., Mouratidou, K., Koidou, E., Panagiotou, A., & Kudlacek, M. (2011). Attitudes of Greek Physical Education Teachers towards Inclusion of Students with Disabilities in Physical Education Classes. *International Journal of Special Education, 26*(1), 1-11.

Dowling, S., McConkey, R., & Hassan, D. (2014). 15 Sport as a vehicle for change in the lives of people with intellectual disabilities. *Sport, Coaching and Intellectual Disability*, 251.

Downs, S. J., Knowles, Z. R., Fairclough, S. J., Heffernan, N., Whitehead, S., Halliwell, S., & Boddy, L. M. (2014). Exploring teachers' perceptions on physical activity engagement for children and young people with intellectual disabilities. *European Journal of Special Needs Education, 29*(3), 402-414.

DuPaul, G. J., & Jimerson, S. R. (2014). Assessing, understanding, and supporting students with

ADHD at school: Contemporary science, practice, and policy.

Durkin, K., Boyle, J., Hunter, S., & Conti-Ramsden, G. (2015). Video games for children and adolescents with special educational needs. *Zeitschrift für Psychologie*.

Dutton, J. (2016). ADHD Athletes: inspiring sports stars with attention deficit. *Attitude strategies and support ADHD & LD*. Retrieved from http://www. additudemag.com/adhd/article.

Dworkin, S. L. (2012). Sample size policy for qualitative studies using in-depth interviews. Archives of Sexual Behavior, 41, 1319-1320. http://dx.doi.org/10.1007 /s10508-012- 0016-6

Eagly, A. H., & Chaiken, S. (1998). Attitude structure and function.

Edwards, J. U., Mauch, L., & Winkelman, M. R. (2011). Relationship of nutrition and physical activity behaviors and fitness measures to academic performance for sixth graders in a Midwest city school district. *Journal of School Health, 81*(2), 65-73.

Eime, R. M., Young, J. A., Harvey, J. T., Charity, M. J., & Payne, W. R. (2013). A systematic review of the psychological and social benefits of participation in sport for children and adolescents: informing development of a conceptual model of health through sport. *Int J Behav Nutr Phys Act, 10*(98), 1.

Eklund, R. C., & Tenenbaum, G. (Eds.). (2014). *Encyclopedia of sport and exercise psychology*. Sage Publications.

El Ansari, W. (2011). When meanings blur, do differences matter? Initiatives for improving the quality and integration of care: conceptual matrix or measurement maze?. *Journal of Integrated Care, 19*(3), 5-21.

Elliott, R. (1930). Modern trends in physical education. *Research Quarterly. American Physical Education Association, 1*(2), 74-85.

Elo, S., Kääriäinen, M., Kanste, O., Pölkki, T., Utriainen, K., & Kyngäs, H. (2014). Qualitative content analysis. *Sage Open, 4*(1), 2158244014522633.

Emerson, E., Einfeld, S., & Stancliffe, R. J. (2010). The mental health of young children with intellectual disabilities or borderline intellectual functioning. *Social psychiatry and psychiatric epidemiology, 45*(5), 579-587.

Emerson, E., Hatton, C., Robertson, J., & Baines, S. (2015). Exposure to second hand tobacco smoke at home and child smoking at age 11 among British children with and without intellectual disability. *Journal of Intellectual Disability Research.*

Emporia State University. (2016). Learning domains: cognitive, affective, psychomotor. Retrieved from https://www.emporia.edu/studentlife/learning-and- assessment/guide/domains.html

Esteban-Cornejo, I., Tejero-González, C. M., Martinez-Gomez, D., Cabanas-Sánchez, V., Fernández-Santos, J. R., Conde-Caveda, J., & Veiga, O. L. (2014). Objectively measured physical activity has a negative but weak association with academic performance in children and adolescents. *Acta Paediatrica, 103*(11), e501-e506.

Eunice Kennedy Shriver National Institute of Child Health and Human Development. (2014). *What are the indicators of learning disabilities?* Retrieved from https://www.nichd.nih.gov/health/topics/learning/conditioninfo/Pages/symptoms.aspx

Everhart, B., Dimon, C., Stone, D., Desmond, D., & Casilio, M. (2012). The influence of daily structured physical activity on academic progress of elementary students with intellectual disabilities. *Education, 133*(2), 298-312.

Evenson, K. R., Ballard, K., Lee, G., & Ammerman, A. (2009). Implementation of a School-Based State Policy to Increase Physical Activity. *Journal of School Health, 79*(5), 231-238.

Fagrell, B., Larsson, H., & Redelius, K. (2012). The game within the game: girls' underperforming position in Physical Education. *Gender and Education, 24*(1), 101-118.

Faison-Hodge, J., & Porretta, D. L. (2004). Physical activity levels of students with mental retardation and students without disabilities. *Adapted Physical Activity Quarterly, 21*(2), 139-152.

Falkner, B., DeLoach, S., Keith, S. W., & Gidding, S. S. (2013). High risk blood pressure and obesity increase the risk for left ventricular hypertrophy in African-American adolescents. *The Journal of pediatrics, 162*(1), 94-100.

Fedewa, A. L., & Ahn, S. (2011). The effects of physical activity and physical fitness on children's achievement and cognitive outcomes: a meta-analysis. *Research quarterly for exercise and sport*, *82*(3), 521-535.

Fink, E., Deighton, J., Humphrey, N., & Wolpert, M. (2015). Assessing the bullying and victimisation experiences of children with special educational needs in mainstream schools: Development and validation of the Bullying Behaviour and Experience Scale. *Research in developmental disabilities*, *36*, 611-619.

Fink, L. D. (2013). *Creating significant learning experiences: An integrated approach to designing college courses*. John Wiley & Sons.

Finn, C. E., Rotherham, A. J., Hokanson, C. R., Will, M. (2001) Rethinking special education. *Thomas B. Fordham Foundation and the Progressive Policy Institute*. Retrieved from http://www.cesa7.org/sped/Parents/ASMT%20Advocacy/wl/spedfinl.pdf

Fisher, W. W., Piazza, C. C., & Roane, H. S. (Eds.). (2011). *Handbook of applied behavior analysis*. Guilford Press.

Fitzgerald, H., & Stride, A. (2012). Stories about physical education from young people with disabilities. *International Journal of Disability, Development and Education*, *59*(3), 283- 293.

Fjørtoft, I., Pedersen, A. V., Sigmundsson, H., & Vereijken, B. (2011). Measuring physical fitness in children who are 5 to 12 years old with a test battery that is functional and easy to administer. *Physical therapy*, *91*(7), 1087-1095.

Flaes, S. A. B., Chinapaw, M. J., Koolhaas, C. M., van Mechelen, W., & Verhagen, E. A. (2015). More children more active: Tailored playgrounds positively affect physical activity levels amongst youth. *Journal of Science and Medicine in Sport*.

Flegal, K. M., Carroll, M. D., Kit, B. K., & Ogden, C. L. (2012). Prevalence of obesity and trends in the distribution of body mass index among US adults, 1999-2010. *Jama*, *307*(5), 491-497.

Flick, U. (2009). *An introduction to qualitative research*. Sage.

Flodmark, C. E., Marcus, C., & Britton, M. (2006). Interventions to prevent obesity in children and adolescents: a systematic literature review. *International journal of obesity*, *30*(4), 579-589.

Flory, S. B., & McCaughtry, N. (2011). Culturally relevant physical education in urban schools: Reflecting cultural knowledge. *Research Quarterly for Exercise and Sport*, *82*(1), 49-60.

Fox, C. K., Barr-Anderson, D., Neumark-Sztainer, D., & Wall, M. (2010). Physical activity and sports team participation: Associations with academic outcomes in middle school and high school students. *Journal of School Health, 80*(1), 31-37.

Fradkin, C., Wallander, J. L., Elliott, M. N., Cuccaro, P., & Schuster, M. A. (2014). Regular physical activity has differential association with reduced obesity among diverse youth in the United States. *Journal of health psychology,* 1359105314559622.

Frederick, C. B., Snellman, K., & Putnam, R. D. (2014). Increasing socioeconomic disparities in adolescent obesity. *Proceedings of the National Academy of Sciences, 111*(4), 1338-1342.

Frey, G. & Stanish, H. I. (2008), Physical activity of youth with intellectual disability: review and research agenda. *Adapt Phys Activ Q.* Temple VA.

Froiland, J. M., Oros, E., Smith, L., & Hirchert, T. (2012). Intrinsic motivation to learn: The nexus between psychological health and academic success. *Contemporary School Psychology: Formerly" The California School Psychologist",* *16*(1), 91-100.

Gable, R. K., & Wolf, M. B. (2012). *Instrument development in the affective domain: Measuring attitudes and values in corporate and school settings* (Vol. 36). Springer Science & Business Media.

Gaddes, W. H. (2013). *Learning disabilities and brain function: A neuropsychological approach.* Springer Science & Business Media.

Gapin, J. I., Labban, J. D., & Etnier, J. L. (2011). The effects of physical activity on attention deficit hyperactivity disorder symptoms: the evidence. *Preventive Medicine, 52,* S70-S74.

Gay, L. R., Mills, G. E., & Airasian, P. W. (2011). *Educational research: Competencies for analysis and applications.* Pearson Higher Ed.

Geidne, S., & Jerlinder, K. (2016). How sports clubs include children and adolescents with disabilities in their activities. A systematic search of peer-reviewed articles. *Sport Science Review, 25*(1-2), 29-52.

Gokdere, M. (2012). A Comparative Study of the Attitude, Concern, and Interaction Levels of Elementary School Teachers and Teacher Candidates towards Inclusive Education. *Educational Sciences: Theory and Practice, 12*(4), 2800-2806.

Gråstén, A., Jaakkola, T., Liukkonen, J., Watt, A., & Yli-Piipari, S. (2012). Prediction of enjoyment in school physical education. *Journal of sports science & medicine, 11*(2), 260.

Gregoriadis, A., Grammatikopoulos, V., & Zachopoulou, E. (2013). Evaluating preschoolers' social skills: The impact of a physical education program from the parents' perspective. *International Journal of Humanities and Social Science, 3*(10), 40-51.

Grenier, M. A. (2011). Coteaching in physical education: A strategy for inclusive practice. *Adapted Physical Activity Quarterly, 28*(2), 95-112.

Grondhuis, S. N., & Aman, M. G. (2014). Overweight and obesity in youth with developmental disabilities: a call to action. *Journal of intellectual disability Research, 58*(9), 787-799.

Guest, G., Bunce, A., & Johnson, L. (2006). How many interviews are enough? An experiment with data saturation and variability. *Field methods, 18*(1), 59-82.

Haapala, E. A. (2013). Cardiorespiratory fitness and motor skills in relation to cognition and academic performance in children—a review. *Journal of human kinetics, 36*(1), 55-68.

Haegele, J. A., & Sutherland, S. (2015). Perspectives of students with disabilities toward physical education: A qualitative inquiry review. *Quest, 67*(3), 255-273.

Haerens, L., Aelterman, N., Van den Berghe, L., De Meyer, J., Soenens, B., & Vansteenkiste, M. (2013). Observing physical education teachers' need-supportive interactions in classroom settings. *Journal of Sport and Exercise Psychology, 35*(1), 3-17.

Haerens, L., Kirk, D., Cardon, G., & De Bourdeaudhuij, I. (2011). Toward the development of a pedagogical model for health-based physical education. *Quest, 63*(3), 321-338.

Haight, W., Kayama, M., Kincaid, T., Evans, K., & Kim, N. K. (2013). The elementary-school functioning of children with maltreatment histories and mild cognitive or behavioral disabilities: A mixed methods inquiry. *Children and Youth Services Review, 35*(3), 420- 428.

Hammel, A. M., & Hourigan, R. M. (2011). *Teaching music to students with special needs: A label-free approach*. Oxford University Press.

Harada, C. M., Siperstein, G. N., Parker, R. C., & Lenox, D. (2011). Promoting social inclusion for people with intellectual disabilities through sport: Special Olympics International, global sport initiatives and strategies. *Sport in Society, 14*(9), 1131-1148.

Harvey, W. J., & Reid, G. (2003). Attention-deficit/hyperactivity disorder: A review of research on movement skill performance and physical fitness. *Adapted Physical Activity Quarterly, 20(1),* 1-25.

Harvey, W. J., Reid, G., Bloom, G. A., Staples, K., Grizenko, N., Mbekou, V., & Joober, R. (2009). Physical activity experiences of boys with and without ADHD. *Adapted Physical Activity Quarterly, 26*(2), 131.

Harwell, J. M., & Jackson, R. W. (2014). *The complete learning disabilities handbook: Ready- to-use strategies and activities for teaching students with learning disabilities.* John Wiley & Sons.

Hatch, J. A. (2002). *Doing qualitative research in education settings.* Suny Press.

Hayakawa, K., & Kobayashi, K. (2011). Physical and motor skill training for children with intellectual disabilities 1, 2, 3. *Perceptual and motor skills, 112*(2), 573-580.

Heidorn, B., & Welch, M. M. (2010). Teaching affective qualities in physical education. *Strategies, 23*(5), 16-21.

Henry, F. M. (1964). Physical education: An academic discipline. *Journal of Health, Physical Education, Recreation, 35*(7), 32-69.

Hills, L. (2007). Friendship, physicality, and physical education: an exploration of the social and embodied dynamics of girls' physical education experiences. *Sport, education and society, 12*(3), 317-336.

Hinckson, E. A., & Curtis, A. (2013). Measuring physical activity in children and youth living with intellectual disabilities: a systematic review. *Research in developmental disabilities, 34*(1), 72-86.

Hinckson, E. A., Dickinson, A., Water, T., Sands, M., & Penman, L. (2013). Physical activity, dietary habits and overall health in overweight and obese children and youth with intellectual disability or autism. *Research in developmental disabilities, 34*(4), 1170-1178.

Hoffman, A. (2003). Teaching decision making to students with learning disabilities by promoting self-determination. *Ericdigest on disabilities and gifted education.* Retrieved from http://www.ericdigests.org/2004-2/self.html

Holt, B. J., & Hannon, J. C. (2006). Teaching-learning in the affective domain. *Strategies, 20*(1), 11-13.

Holt, N. L. (Ed.). (2016). *Positive youth development through sport.* Routledge.

Horowitz, S.H., (2014) Behavior problems and learning disabilities. *National center for learning disabilities.* Retrieved from http://www.ncld.org/parents-child- disabilities/ social-emotional-skills/behavior-problems-learning-disabilities

Howie, E. K., & Pate, R. R. (2012). Physical activity and academic achievement in children: A historical perspective. *Journal of Sport and Health Science, 1*(3), 160-169.

Hsieh, K., Rimmer, J. H., & Heller, T. (2014). Obesity and associated factors in adults with intellectual disability. *Journal of Intellectual Disability Research, 58*(9), 851-863.

Hulett, K. E. (2009). Legal Aspects of Special Education. Upper Saddle River, NJ: Pearson Education Inc.

Hünük, D., & Demirhan, G. (2010). Turkish adolescents' attitudes toward physical education. *Perceptual and motor skills, 111*(2), 324-332.

Hutchinson, N., Minnes, P., Burbidge, J., Dods, J., Pyle, A., & Dalton, C. J. (2015). Perspectives of Canadian Teacher Candidates on Inclusion of Children with Developmental Disabilities: A Mixed-Methods Study. *Exceptionality Education International, 25*(2).

Hwang, Y. S., & Evans, D. (2011). Attitudes towards inclusion: gaps between belief and practice. *International Journal of Special Education, 26*(1), 136-146.

Ilmer, S., Elliott, S., Snyder, J. A., Nahan, N., & Colombo, M. (2005). Analysis of urban teachers' 1st year experiences in an alternative certification program. *Action in Teacher Education, 27*(1), 3-14.

Jaakkola, T., Wang, C. J., Soini, M., & Liukkonen, J. (2015). Students' perceptions of motivational climate and enjoyment in Finnish physical education: A latent profile analysis. *Journal of sports science & medicine, 14*(3), 477.

James, A. R., Kellman, M., & Lieberman, L. (2011). Perspectives on inclusion from students with disabilities and responsive strategies for teachers. *Journal of Physical Education, Recreation & Dance, 82*(1), 33-54.

Jerlinder, K., Danermark, B., & Gill, P. (2010). Swedish primary-school teachers' attitudes to inclusion–the case of PE and pupils with physical disabilities. *European Journal of Special Needs Education, 25*(1), 45-57.

Jones, J. L., & Hensley, L. R. (2012). Taking a closer look at the impact of classroom placement: Students share their perspective from inside special education classrooms. *Educational Research Quarterly, 35*(3), 33.

Jones, M. M., Harrison, B., Harp, B., & Sheppard-Jones, K. (2016). Teaching college students with intellectual disability: what faculty members say about the experience. *Inclusion, 4*(2), 89-108.

Johnson, G. B. (1942). A study of the relationship that exists between physical skill as measured, and the general intelligence of college students. *Research Quarterly. American Association for Health, Physical Education and Recreation, 13*(1), 57-59.

Kamath, C. C., Vickers, K. S., Ehrlich, A., McGovern, L., Johnson, J., Singhal, V., & Montori, V. M. (2008). Behavioral interventions to prevent childhood obesity: a systematic review and metaanalyses of randomized trials. *The Journal of Clinical Endocrinology & Metabolism, 93*(12), 4606-4615.

Kamtsios, S. (2010). Gender differences in elementary school children in perceived athletic competence, body attractiveness, attitudes towards exercise and participation in physical activity. *International Quarterly of Sport Science, 2*, 2010.

Kamtsios, S. (2012). Sources of stress and stages of change for stress management in school age children: proposals for points of intervention. *Scientific Journal of Pure and Applied Sciences, 1*(3), 133-143.

Kantomaa, M. T., Stamatakis, E., Kankaanpää, A., Kaakinen, M., Rodriguez, A., Taanila, A., & Tammelin, T. (2013). Physical activity and obesity mediate the association between childhood motor function and adolescents' academic achievement. *Proceedings of the National Academy of Sciences, 110*(5), 1917-1922.

Karnik, S., & Kanekar, A. (2015). Childhood obesity: a global public health crisis. *Int J Prev Med, 2012. 3 (1)*, 1-7.

Katzmarzyk, P. T., Barreira, T. V., Broyles, S. T., Champagne, C. M., Chaput, J. P., Fogelholm, M., & Lambert, E. V. (2013). The international study of childhood obesity, lifestyle and the environment (ISCOLE): Design and methods. *BMC Public Health, 13*(1), 1.

Kelder, S. H., Springer, A. E., Barroso, C. S., Smith, C. L., Sanchez, E., Ranjit, N., & Hoelscher, D. M. (2009). Implementation of Texas Senate Bill 19 to increase physical activity in elementary schools. *Journal of Public Health Policy, 30*(1), S221-S247.

Kelly, S. A., Melnyk, B. M., Jacobson, D. L., & O'Haver, J. A. (2011). Correlates among healthy lifestyle cognitive beliefs, healthy lifestyle choices, social support, and healthy behaviors in adolescents: Implications for behavioral change strategies and future research. *Journal of pediatric health care, 25*(4), 216-223.

Kim, J. R. (2011). Influence of teacher preparation programmes on preservice teachers' attitudes toward inclusion. *International Journal of Inclusive Education, 15*(3), 355-377.

Kimiecik, J. C., & Horn, T. S. (2016). The big motivational picture: Examining the relationship between positive intrapersonal processes and adolescent health-promoting behaviors. *Applied Developmental Science*, 1-16.

King, M., Shields, N., Imms, C., Black, M., & Ardern, C. (2013). Participation of children with intellectual disability compared with typically developing children. *Research in developmental disabilities, 34*(5), 1854-1862.

Kirk, D. (2014). *Physical Education and Curriculum Study (Routledge Revivals): A Critical Introduction*. Routledge.

Kirk, H. E., Gray, K., Riby, D. M., & Cornish, K. M. (2015). Cognitive training as a resolution for early executive function difficulties in children with intellectual disabilities. *Research in developmental disabilities, 38*, 145-160.

Kjønniksen, L., Fjørtoft, I., & Wold, B. (2009). Attitude to physical education and participation in organized youth sports during adolescence related to physical activity in young adulthood: A 10-year longitudinal study. *European Physical Education Review, 15*(2), 139-154.

Klaviņa, A., & Strazdiņa, N. (2015). Professional Attitude of Physical Education Teachers toward Education Process of Students with Severe Intellectual Disabilities. In *society, integration, education. Proceedings of the International Scientific Conference* (Vol. 3, pp. 558-566).

Kohl III, H. W., & Cook, H. D. (Eds.). (2013). *Educating the student body: Taking physical activity and physical education to school*. National Academies Press.

Kohl, H. W., Craig, C. L., Lambert, E. V., Inoue, S., Alkandari, J. R., Leetongin, G., & Lancet Physical Activity Series Working Group. (2012). The pandemic of physical inactivity: global action for public health. *The Lancet, 380*(9838), 294-305.

Korbel, D. M., Lucia, J. H., Wenzel, C. M., & Anderson, B. G. (2011). Collaboration strategies to facilitate successful transition of students with disabilities in a changing higher education environment. *New Directions for Higher Education, 2011*(154), 17-25.

Kriemler, S., Meyer, U., Martin, E., Van Sluijs, E. M. F., Andersen, L. B., & Martin, B. W. (2011). Effect of school-based interventions on physical activity and fitness in children and adolescents: a review of reviews and systematic update. *British journal of sports medicine, 45*(11), 923-930.

Kurková, P., Nemček, D., & Labudová, J. (2015). Pupils with sensory disabilities in physical education classes: Attitudes and preferences. *Acta Gymnica, 45*(3), 139-145.

Kvale, S. (2008). *Doing interviews*. Sage.

Lai, S. K., Costigan, S. A., Morgan, P. J., Lubans, D. R., Stodden, D. F., Salmon, J., & Barnett, L. M. (2014). Do school-based interventions focusing on physical activity, fitness, or fundamental movement skill competency produce a sustained impact in these outcomes in children and adolescents? A systematic review of follow-up studies. *Sports Medicine, 44*(1), 67-79.

Lavay, B., French, R., & Henderson, H. (2015). *Positive Behavior Management in Physical Activity Settings, 3E.* Human Kinetics.

Lawton, K. E., Gerdes, A. C., Haack, L. M., & Schneider, B. (2014). Acculturation, cultural values, and Latino parental beliefs about the etiology of ADHD. *Administration and Policy in Mental Health and Mental Health Services Research, 41*(2), 189-204.

Lewis, B. A., Williams, D. M., Frayeh, A., & Marcus, B. H. (2016). Self-efficacy versus perceived enjoyment as predictors of physical activity behaviour. *Psychology & health, 31*(4), 456-469.

Li, Z., & Sun, C. (2013). Reflections on curriculum resources and its development and utilization: social capital perspective. *Global Education, 42*(9), 11-17.

Lin, J. D., Lin, P. Y., Lin, L. P., Chang, Y. Y., Wu, S. R., & Wu, J. L. (2010). Physical activity and its determinants among adolescents with intellectual disabilities. *Research in developmental disabilities, 31*(1), 263-269.

Linton, S., (1998). *Claiming Disability: Knowledge and Identity.* New York: New York University Press.

Liu, W., Wang, J., & Xu, F. (2008). Middle school children's attitudes toward physical activity. *The ICHPER-SD Journal of Research in Health, Physical Education, Recreation, Sport & Dance, 3*(2), 78.

Llewellyn, G., Emerson, E., Honey, A., & Kariuki, M. (2013). Left behind: monitoring the social inclusion of young Australians with self-reported long term health conditions, impairments or disabilities 2001-2009.

Lloyd, L. J., Langley-Evans, S. C., & McMullen, S. (2012). Childhood obesity and risk of the adult metabolic syndrome: a systematic review. *International journal of obesity, 36*(1), 1- 11.

Lohman, A. E. (2011). *Special education learning environments: Inclusion versus self-contained* Lindenwood University.

London School of Economics. (2016). How do I report my qualitative data? Retrieved from http://www.lse.ac.uk/media@lse/research/

Lotan, M., Hadash, R., Amrani, S., Pinsker, A., & Weiss, T. P. (2015). Improving balance of individuals with intellectual and developmental disability through a virtual reality intervention program. *Palaestra, 29*(4).

MacFarlane, K., & Woolfson, L. M. (2013). Teacher attitudes and behavior toward the inclusion of children with social, emotional and behavioral difficulties in mainstream schools: An application of the theory of planned behavior. *Teaching and teacher education, 29*, 46-52.

Mahony, P. (2012). *Schools for the boys?: co-education reassessed* (Vol. 72). Routledge

Mandell, D.S., Davis, J.K., Bevans, K., & Guevara, J.P. (2009). Ethnic disparities in special education labeling among children with attention deficit/hyperactivity disorder. Journal of Emotional and Behavioral Disorders. Vol. 16, (1). Retrieved from http://proquest.umi.com.proxy1. ncu.edu/pqdweb/

Mansell, J., & Beadle-Brown, J. (2012). *Active support: Enabling and empowering people with intellectual disabilities.* Jessica Kingsley Publishers.

Mărgăriţoiu, A. (2015). Teachers' Commitment from Special-need Schools–A Predictor of their Humanity and Loyalty. *Procedia-Social and Behavioral Sciences, 203,* 322-326.

Mason, M. (2010). Sample size and saturation in PhD studies using qualitative interviews. In *Forum qualitative Sozialforschung/Forum: qualitative social research* (Vol. 11, No. 3).

May, A. L., Freedman, D., Sherry, B., Blanck, H. M., & Centers for Disease Control and Prevention (CDC). (2013). Obesity—United States, 1999–2010. *MMWR Surveill Summ, 62*(Suppl 3), 120-128.

McConkey, R., Dowling, S., Hassan, D., & Menke, S. (2013). Promoting social inclusion through Unified Sports for youth with intellectual disabilities: a five-nation study. *Journal of intellectual disability research, 57*(10), 923-935.

McGillivray, J., McVilly, K., Skouteris, H., & Boganin, C. (2013). Parental factors associated with obesity in children with disability: a systematic review. *Obesity Reviews, 14*(7), 541- 554.

McKenzie, T. L., & Lounsbery, M. A. (2013). Physical education teacher effectiveness in a public health context. *Research quarterly for exercise and sport, 84*(4), 419-430.

McLeskey, J. M., Rosenberg, M. S., & Westling, D. L. (2012). *Inclusion: Effective practices for all students.* Pearson Higher Ed.

McMillan, J. H., & Schumacher, S. (2014). *Research in education: Evidence-based inquiry.* Pearson Higher Ed.

McPherson, A. C., Keith, R., & Swift, J. A. (2014). Obesity prevention for children with physical disabilities: a scoping review of physical activity and nutrition interventions. *Disability and rehabilitation, 36*(19), 1573-1587.

Mercier, K., Phillips, S., & Silverman, S. (2016). High School Physical Education Teachers' Attitudes and use of Fitness Tests. *The High School Journal, 99*(2), 179-190.

Merikangas, K. R., & He, J. (2014). Epidemiology of mental disorders in children and adolescents. *From Research to Practice in Child and Adolescent Mental Health*, 19.

Merriam, S. B., & Tisdell, E. J. (2015). *Qualitative research: A guide to design and implementation*. John Wiley & Sons.

Michael, C., & Marcus, L. (2015). Relationship between quality of life and resilience among sport-active Singaporean youth. *Physical education of students, 2*.

Milsom, A. (2006). Creating Positive School Experiences for Students with Disabilities. Professional School Counseling Journal, October 2006, 10(1), 66-72.

Missiuna, C., Cairney, J., Pollock, N., Campbell, W., Russell, D. J., Macdonald, K., & Cousins, M. (2014). Psychological distress in children with developmental coordination disorder and attention-deficit hyperactivity disorder. *Research in developmental disabilities, 35*(5), 1198-1207.

Moore, R. D., Drollette, E. S., Scudder, M. R., Bharij, A., & Hillman, C. H. (2014). The influence of cardiorespiratory fitness on strategic, behavioral, and electrophysiological indices of arithmetic cognition in preadolescent children. *Frontiers in human neuroscience, 8*.

Moren. A. (2017). Understanding your child's trouble with impulsivity. *Understood*. Retrieved from https://www.understood.org/en/learning-attention-issues/child-learning-disabilities/

Morley, D., Bailey, R., Tan, J., & Cooke, B. (2005). Inclusive physical education: Teachers' views of including pupils with special educational needs and/or disabilities in physical education. *European Physical Education Review, 11*(1), 84-107.

Morse, J. M. (2010). Sampling in grounded theory. *The Sage handbook of grounded theory*, 229-244.

Moustakas, C. (1994). *Phenomenological research methods*. Sage Publications.

Mozaffarian, D., Afshin, A., Benowitz, N. L., Bittner, V., Daniels, S. R., Franch, H. A. & Zakai, N. A. (2012). Population Approaches to Improve Diet, Physical Activity, and Smoking Habits A Scientific Statement From the American Heart Association. *Circulation, 126*(12), 1514-1563.

Murdick, N. L., Gartin, B. L., & Fowler, G. A. (2013). *Special education law*. Pearson Higher Ed.

Naaldenberg, J., Kuijken, N., van Dooren, K., & de Valk, H. V. S. L. (2013). Topics, methods and challenges in health promotion for people with intellectual disabilities: a structured review of literature. *Research in developmental disabilities, 34*(12), 4534-4545.

National Association for Sports and Physical Education. (2016). NASPE set the standards. Physical education as an academic subject. Retrieved from https://www.sophe.org/Sophe/PDF/Summer%20Webinar%20Series

National Association for Sport and Physical Education [NASPE] (2004). *Moving Into the Future: National Standards for Physical Education.* 2nd ed. Reston, VA.

National Association for Sport and Physical Education [NASPE] (2006). Teaching large class sizes in physical education guidelines and strategies. Retrieved from http://www.shapeamerica.org/publications/resources/teachingtools/qualitype/

National Association for Sport and Physical Education [NASPE] (2011). Active Start: A Statement of Physical Activity Guidelines for Children from Birth to Age 5 (2nd ed.). Reston, VA: NASPE. Retrieved from http://columbus.gov/uploadedFiles/Public_Health/Content_Editors/Planning_and_Perfor mance/Healthy_Children_Healthy_Weights/NASPE

National Association for Sports and Physical Education. (2014). National standards for physical education. Retrieved from www.naspe.org/nationalstandards

National Association for Sports and Physical Education. (2016). Physical education as an academic subject. Retrieved from www.naspe.org/ physical education/academics

National Center for Educational Statistics. (2014). Children and youth with disabilities. Retrieved from http://nces.ed.gov/programs/coe/indicator_cgg.asp

National Center for Educational Statistics. (2015). Common Core of Data. Retrieved from http://nces.ed.gov/ccd/districtsearch/district

National Center for Health Statistics, Centers for Disease Control, & Prevention (Eds.). (2015). *Health, United States, 2013, with special feature on prescription drugs.* Government Printing Office.

National Dissemination Center for Children with Disabilities. (2012). Categories of disabilities under IDEA. Retrieved from http://www.parentcenterhub.org/wp

National Institute of Mental Health. (2016). Attention deficit Hyperactivity Disorder. Retrieved from http://www.nimh.nih.gov/health/topics/attention-deficit-hyperactivity-disorder

Nelson, T. D., Benson, E. R., & Jensen, C. D. (2010). Negative attitudes toward physical activity: Measurement and role in predicting physical activity levels among preadolescents. *Journal of pediatric psychology, 35*(1), 89-98.

Newcombe, S. (2011). A Social History of Yoga and Ayurveda in Britain, 1950-1995. University of Cambridge.

New York Department of Education. (2014). Special education services. Retrieved from http://schools.nyc.gov/documents/d75/iep/ContinuumServices.pdf

Ng, M., Fleming, T., Robinson, M., Thomson, B., Graetz, N., Margono, C., & Abraham, J. P. (2014). Global, regional, and national prevalence of overweight and obesity in children and adults during 1980–2013: a systematic analysis for the Global Burden of Disease Study 2013. *The Lancet, 384*(9945), 766-781.

Nowicki, E. A., & Sandieson, R. (2002). A meta-analysis of school-age children's attitudes towards persons with physical or intellectual disabilities. *International Journal of Disability, Development and Education, 49*(3), 243-265.

Nunlist, C. A. (2013). *The Relationship Between Physical Activity and Academic Performance* (Doctoral dissertation, The Evergreen State College).

Obrusnikova, I. (2008). Physical educators 1 beliefs about teaching children with disabilities1. *Perceptual and motor skills, 106*(2), 637-644.

O'Dare, K. (2011). *Environmental sprawl and weight status: The paradox of obesity in the food desert.* The Florida State University.

Odom, S. L., Buysse, V., & Soukakou, E. (2011). Inclusion for young children with disabilities: A quarter century of research perspectives. *Journal of Early Intervention, 33*(4), 344-356.

Office of Disease Prevention and Health Promotion. (2016). Physical activity guidelines advisory committee report. Retrieved from https://health.gov/PAGuidelines/report/C_keyterms.aspx

Office of the Surgeon General. (2010). Childhood overweight and obesity prevention initiative. Retrieved from http://www.surgeongeneral.gov/obesityprevention/index.html

Ogden, C. L., Carroll, M. D., Kit, B. K., & Flegal, K. M. (2014). Prevalence of obesity in the United States, 2011-2012.

Olds, T., Maher, C., Zumin, S., Péneau, S., Lioret, S., Castetbon, K., & Lissner, L. (2011). Evidence that the prevalence of childhood overweight is plateauing: data from nine countries. *International Journal of Pediatric Obesity, 6*(5-6), 342-360.

Orlić, A., Pejčić, B., Lazarević, D., & Milanović, I. (2016). The predictors of students' attitude towards inclusion of children with disabilities in physical education classes. *Fizička kultura, 70*(2), 126-134.

Özer, D., Nalbant, S., Ağlamış, E., Baran, F., Kaya Samut, P., Aktop, A., & Hutzler, Y. (2013). Physical education teachers' attitudes towards children with intellectual disability: the impact of time in service, gender, and previous acquaintance. *Journal of Intellectual Disability Research, 57*(11), 1001-1013.

Ozmun, J. C., & Gallahue, D. L. (2016). Motor development. *Adapted Physical Education and Sport, 6E,* 375.

Pahlke, E., Hyde, J. S., & Allison, C. M. (2014). The effects of single-sex compared with coeducational schooling on students' performance and attitudes: A meta-analysis. *Psychological Bulletin, 140*(4), 1042.

Pan, C. Y., Liu, C. W., Chung, I. C., & Hsu, P. J. (2015). Physical activity levels of adolescents with and without intellectual disabilities during physical education and recess. *Research in developmental disabilities, 36,* 579-586.

Palisano, R. J., Chiarello, L. A., King, G. A., Novak, I., Stoner, T., & Fiss, A. (2012). Participation-based therapy for children with physical disabilities. *Disability and Rehabilitation, 34*(12), 1041-1052.

Pence, A. R., & Dymond, S. K. (2016). Teachers' beliefs about the participation of students with severe disabilities in school clubs. *Research and Practice for Persons with Severe Disabilities,* 1540796915626009.

Phillips, A. C., & Holland, A. J. (2011). Assessment of objectively measured physical activity levels in individuals with intellectual disabilities with and without Down's syndrome. *PLoS One, 6*(12), e28618.

Phillips, K. L., Schieve, L. A., Visser, S., Boulet, S., Sharma, A. J., Kogan, M. D., & Yeargin- Allsopp, M. (2014). Prevalence and impact of unhealthy weight in a national sample of US adolescents with autism and other learning and behavioral disabilities. *Maternal and child health journal, 18*(8), 1964-1975.

Pieters, S., Desoete, A., Roeyers, H., Vanderswalmen, R., & Van Waelvelde, H. (2012). Behind mathematical learning disabilities: What about visual perception and motor skills?

Pindus, D. M., Drollette, E. S., Scudder, M. R., Khan, N. A., Raine, L. B., Sherar, L. B., & Hillman, C. H. (2016). Moderate-to-Vigorous Physical Activity, Indices of Cognitive Control, and Academic Achievement in Preadolescents. *The Journal of pediatrics.*

Learning and Individual Differences, 22(4), 498-504.

Polanczyk, G. V., Willcutt, E. G., Salum, G. A., Kieling, C., & Rohde, L. A. (2014). ADHD prevalence estimates across three decades: an updated systematic review and meta- regression analysis. *International journal of epidemiology, 43*(2), 434-442.

Pontifex, M. B., Saliba, B. J., Raine, L. B., Picchietti, D. L., & Hillman, C. H. (2013). Exercise improves behavioral, neurocognitive, and scholastic performance in children with attention-deficit/hyperactivity disorder. *The Journal of pediatrics*, *162*(3), 543-551.

Public Broadcasting Service [PBS]. 2002. Misunderstood minds. Retrieved from http://www.pbs.org/wgbh/misunderstoodminds/attentiondiffs.html

Rarick, G. (Ed.). (2012). *Physical activity: Human growth and development*. Elsevier.

Rasberry, C. N., Lee, S. M., Robin, L., Laris, B. A., Russell, L. A., Coyle, K. K., & Nihiser, A. J. (2011). The association between school-based physical activity, including physical education, and academic performance: a systematic review of the literature. *Preventive medicine*, *52*, S10-S20.

Raza, K. K., Afridi, A. K., & Ali, A. (2013). The contribution of regional institutes for in- service teachers training: a study from Khyber PakhtoonKhwa. *The Dialogue*, *8*(2).

Reinehr, T., Dobe, M., Winkel, K., Schaefer, A., & Hoffmann, D. (2010). Obesity in disabled children and adolescents. *Dtsch Arztebl Int*, *107*(15), 268-275.

Reinke, W. M., Stormont, M., Herman, K. C., Puri, R., & Goel, N. (2011). Supporting children's mental health in schools: Teacher perceptions of needs, roles, and barriers. *School Psychology Quarterly*, *26*(1), 1.

Rice, J. K. (2013). Learning from experience? Evidence on the impact and distribution of teacher experience and the implications for teacher policy. *Education*, *8*(3), 332-348.

Richards, K. A., & Templin, T. J. (2011). The influence of a state mandated induction assistance program on the socialization of a beginning physical education teacher. *Journal of Teaching in Physical Education*, *30*(4), 340-357.

Rimmer, J. H., & Marques, A. C. (2012). Physical activity for people with disabilities. *The Lancet*, *380*(9838), 193-195.

Rimmer, J. H., Riley, B., Wang, E., Rauworth, A., & Jurkowski, J. (2004). Physical activity participation among persons with disabilities: barriers and facilitators. *American journal of preventive medicine*, *26*(5), 419-425.

Robbins, J. M., Mallya, G., Polansky, M., & Schwarz, D. F. (2015). Prevalence, disparities, and trends in obesity and severe obesity among students in the Philadelphia, Pennsylvania, school district, 2006–2010. *The Childhood Obesity Epidemic: Why Are Our Children Obese—And What Can We Do About It?*, 29.

Robinson, O. C. (2014). Sampling in interview-based qualitative research: A theoretical and practical guide. *Qualitative Research in Psychology*, *11*(1), 25-41.

Romney, A., Weller, S., & Batchelder, W. (1986). Culture as consensus: A theory of culture and informant accuracy. *American Anthropologist 88*, 313-338. http://dx.doi.org/10.1111/(ISSN)1548-1433

Roth, K., Zittel, L., Pyfer, J., & Auxter, D. (2016). *Principles and Methods of Adapted Physical Education & Recreation.* Jones & Bartlett Publishers.

Roulston, K. (2010). *Reflective interviewing: A guide to theory and practice.* Thousand Oaks, CA: SAGE Publications.

Rubin, H. J., & Rubin, I. S. (2011). *Qualitative interviewing: The art of hearing data.* Sage.

Sainero, A., del Valle, J. F., López, M., & Bravo, A. (2013). Exploring the specific needs of an understudied group: children with intellectual disability in residential child care. *Children and Youth Services Review, 35*(9), 1393-1399.

Saldaña, J. (2015). *The coding manual for qualitative researchers.* Sage.

Samalot—Rivera, A., Porretta, D. L. (2012). The influence of social skills instruction on sport and game related behaviors of students with emotional or behavioral disorders. *Physical Education and Sport Pedagogy, 17,* 1-16.

Sanchez, B., Byra, M., & Wallhead, T. L. (2012). Students' perceptions of the command, practice, and inclusion styles of teaching. *Physical Education & Sport Pedagogy, 17*(3), 317-330.

Savolainen, H., Engelbrecht, P., Nel, M., & Malinen, O. P. (2012). Understanding teachers' attitudes and self-efficacy in inclusive education: implications for pre-service and in- service teacher education. *European Journal of Special Needs Education, 27*(1), 51-68.

Saunders, M. N. (2012). Choosing research participants. *Qualitative organizational research: Core methods and current challenges,* 35-52.

Serdula, M. K., Ivery, D., Coates, R. J., Freedman, D. S., Williamson, D. F., & Byers, T. (1993). Do obese children become obese adults? A review of the literature. *Preventive medicine, 22*(2), 167-177.

Sermier Dessemontet, R., & Bless, G. (2013). The impact of including children with intellectual disability in general education classrooms on the academic achievement of their low-, average-, and high-achieving peers. *Journal of Intellectual and Developmental Disability, 38*(1), 23-30.

Sewell, M., (2016). University of Arizona. The use of qualitative interviews in evaluation. Retrieve from http://ag.arizona.edu/sfcs/

Scarlett, W. G. (Ed.). (2015). *The SAGE Encyclopedia of Classroom Management.* SAGE Publications.

Schaeffer, E. M. (1891). The revival of physical education and practical hygiene. *The Journal of Nervous and Mental Disease, 16*(8), 504-516.

Schieve, L. A., Gonzalez, V., Boulet, S. L., Visser, S. N., Rice, C. E., Braun, K. V. N., & Boyle, C. A. (2012). Concurrent medical conditions and health care use and needs among children with learning and behavioral developmental disabilities, National Health Interview Survey, 2006–2010. *Research in developmental disabilities, 33*(2), 467-476.

Schlechty, P. C. (2011). *Engaging students: The next level of working on the work.* John Wiley & Sons.

Scholz, M., Gebhardt, M., & Tobias, T. (2012). Attitudes of Student Teachers and Teachers towards Integration–A Short Survey in Bavaria/Germany. *Disability Research Center Journal, 2*(3), 112-156.

Scull, J., & Winkler, A. M. (2011). Shifting Trends in Special Education. *Thomas B. Fordham Institute.*

Shajie, K., Raoof, M., Nayerabadi, M., & Houshyar, K. (2014). Effect of parental attitude toward physical activity on sport participation of their children in school. *Advances in Environmental Biology*, 2211-2216.

Sharma, M. (2016). *Theoretical foundations of health education and health promotion.* Jones & Bartlett Publishers.

Sheehan, D., & Katz, L. (2012). The practical and theoretical implications of flow theory and intrinsic motivation in designing and implementing exergaming in the school environment. *The Journal of the Canadian Game Studies Association, 6*(9), 53-68.

Sheehan, M., Marti, V., & Roberts, T. (2014). Ethical Review of Research on Human Subjects at Unilever: Reflections on Governance. *Bioethics, 28*(6), 284-292.

Shields N, Dodd KJ, Abblitt C. (2009). Do children with Down syndrome perform sufficient physical activity to maintain good health? A pilot study. *Adapted Physical Activity Quarterly 26*(4):307-20.

Shields, N., Synnot, A. J., & Barr, M. (2012). Perceived barriers and facilitators to physical activity for children with disability: a systematic review. *British journal of sports medicine, 46*(14), 989-997.

Shooshtari, S., Brownell, M., Mills, R. S., Dik, N., Yu, D. C., Chateau, D., & Wetzel, M. (2016). Comparing Health Status, Health Trajectories and Use of Health and Social Services between Children with and without Developmental

Disabilities: A Population-based Longitudinal Study in Manitoba. *Journal of Applied Research in Intellectual Disabilities.*

Siemens, G. (2014). Connectivism: A learning theory for the digital age.

Simms, K., Bock, S., & Hackett, L. (2013). Do the duration and frequency of physical education predict academic achievement, self-concept, social skills, food consumption, and body mass index?. *Health Education Journal*, 0017896912471040.

Simpson, G.A., Cohen, R.A., Pastor, P.N., & Reuben, C.A. (2008). Use of mental health services in the past 12 months by children aged 4–17 years: United States, 2005–2006. *NCHS Data Brief, No. 8*, 1-8. Retrieved from http://www.cdc.gov/nchs/data/databriefs/db08.pdf

Singh, A., Uijtdewilligen, L., Twisk, J. W., Van Mechelen, W., & Chinapaw, M. J. (2012). Physical activity and performance at school: a systematic review of the literature including a methodological quality assessment. *Archives of pediatrics & adolescent medicine, 166*(1), 49-55.

Singh, G. K., Kenney, M. K., Ghandour, R. M., Kogan, M. D., & Lu, M. C. (2013). Mental health outcomes in US children and adolescents born prematurely or with low birthweight. *Depression research and treatment, 2013.*

Singh, G. K., Kogan, M. D., & Van Dyck, P. C. (2010). Changes in state-specific childhood obesity and overweight prevalence in the United States from 2003 to 2007. *Archives of pediatrics & adolescent medicine, 164*(7), 598-607.

Skukauskaite, A. (2012). Transparency in transcribing: Making visible theoretical bases impacting knowledge construction from open-ended interview records. In *Forum Qualitative Sozialforschung/Forum: Qualitative Social Research* (Vol. 13, No. 1).

Slater, S. J., Nicholson, L., Chriqui, J., Turner, L., & Chaloupka, F. (2012). The impact of state laws and district policies on physical education and recess practices in a nationally representative sample of US public elementary schools. *Archives of pediatrics & adolescent medicine, 166*(4), 311-316.

Slevin, E., Truesdale-Kennedy, M., McConkey, R., Livingstone, B., & Fleming, P. (2014). Obesity and overweight in intellectual and non-intellectually disabled children. *Journal of Intellectual Disability Research, 58*(3), 211-220.

Smiley, S. (2015). Gender issues in physical education. Retrieved from http://skemman.is/item/view/1946/20591

Smith, A., & Thomas, N. (2006). Including pupils with special educational needs and disabilities in national curriculum physical education: A brief review. *European Journal of Special Needs Education, 21*(1), 69-83.

Smith, D.G., & Associates. (1997). *Diversity works: The emerging picture of how students benefit.* Washington, D.C.: American Association of Colleges and Universities.

Smith, G. A. (2012). Perceptions and evaluation of a physical activity program. ProQuest Dissertations & Theses Global. (1277537719). Retrieved from http://search.proquest.com.proxy1.ncu.edu/docview/1277537719

Smith, J. & Osborn, M. (2007). Pain as an assault on the self: An interpretive phenomenological analysis of the psychological impact of chronic benign low back pain. Psychology and Health, 22(5), 517-534. doi:10.1080/14768320600941756

Smith, M. A., & St Pierre, P. E. (2009). Secondary students' perceptions of enjoyment in physical education: An American and English perspective. *Physical Educator, 66*(4), 209.

Sousa, D. A. (2016). *How the special needs brain learns.* Corwin Press.

Soy, S. (2015). The case study as a research method.

SPARK. (2014). *Academics & physical activities.* Retrieved from http://www.sparkpe.org/physical-education-resources/academics-physical-activity/

SPARK. (2016). *Why It's Crucial For Kids to Enjoy Physical Education.* Retrieved from www.sparkpe.org

Spencer-Cavaliere, N., & Watkinson, E. J. (2010). Inclusion understood from the perspectives of children with disability. *Adapted Physical Activity Quarterly, 27*(4), 275-293.

Stabeno, M. E. (2004). *The ADHD affected athlete.* Trafford Publishing.

Stake, R. E. (2010). *Qualitative research: Studying how things work.* Guilford Press.

Stake, R. E. (2013). *Multiple case study analysis.* Guilford Press.

Standage, M., Gillison, F. B., Ntoumanis, N., & Treasure, D. C. (2012). Predicting students' physical activity and health-related well-being: A prospective cross-domain investigation of motivation across school physical education and exercise settings. *Journal of Sport & Exercise Psychology, 2012*(34), 37-60.

State of New Jersey. (2009). Department of Education. Glossary of acronyms and terms. Retrieved from http://www.state.nj.us/education/genfo/acronyms.pdf

State of New Jersey. (2016). Department of Education. Comprehensive health and physical education. Retrieved from http://www.state.nj.us/education/aps/cccs/chpe/

State of New Jersey. (2016). Department of Education. School development authority. Retrieved from https://www.njsda.gov/njsda/

Strand, B., Knudsen, N., Bower, M., & Swedberg, R. (2013). Ideas to Enhance your K-12 Physical Education Curriculum. *Journal of the Oklahoma Association for Health, Physical Education, Recreation, and Dance, 50*(3), 28-34.

Strean, W. B. (2011). Remembering instructors: pain, play, and pedagogy. Qualitative Research in Sport and Exercise, 1(3), 210-220.doi 10.1080/19398440903192290

Stuckey, H. L. (2014). The first step in Data Analysis: Transcribing and managing qualitative research data. *Journal of Social Health and Diabetes, 2*(1), 6.

Subramaniam, P. R., & Silverman, S. (2000). Validation of scores from an instrument assessing student attitude toward physical education. *Measurement in Physical Education and Exercise Science, 4*(1), 29-43.

Subramaniam, P. R., & Silverman, S. (2007). Middle school students' attitudes toward physical education. *Teaching and Teacher Education, 23*(5), 602-611.

Summerbell, C. D., Waters, E., Edmunds, L. D., Kelly, S., Brown, T., & Campbell, K. J. (2005). Interventions for preventing obesity in children. *Cochrane Database Syst Rev, 3*(3).

Swanson, H. L., & Harris, K. R. (Eds.). (2013). *Handbook of learning disabilities.* Guilford press.

Sykes, H. J. (2011). *Queer bodies: Sexualities, genders, & fatness in physical education* (Vol. 36). Peter Lang.

Tashakkori, A., & Teddlie, C. (Eds.). (2010). *Sage handbook of mixed methods in social & behavioral research.* Sage.

Teddlie, C., & Tashakkori, A. (Eds.). (2009). *Foundations of mixed methods research: Integrating quantitative and qualitative approaches in the social and behavioral sciences.* Sage Publications Inc.

Thomas, G. (2011). A typology for the case study in social science following a review of definition, discourse, and structure. *Qualitative inquiry, 17*(6), 511-521.

Thomas, G. (2015). *How to do your case study.* Sage.

Tindall, D., MacDonald, W., Carroll, E., & Moody, B. (2014). Pre-service teachers' attitudes towards children with disabilities An Irish perspective. *European Physical Education Review,* 1356336X14556861.

Torres-Luque, G., Beltrán, J., Calahorro, F., López-Fernández, I., & Nikolaidis, P. T. (2016). Analysis of the distribution of physical activity in early childhood education students. *Cuadernos de Psicología del Deporte, 16*(1), 261-267.

Townsend, C. E. (2011). Developing a comprehensive research agenda for people with intellectual disability to inform policy development and reform. *Journal of Policy and Practice in Intellectual Disabilities, 8*(2), 113-124.

Townsend, J. R. (2008). *Attitudes of Students Without Disabilities Toward Students with Disabilities.* St. Ambrose University.

Tremblay, M. S., LeBlanc, A. G., Kho, M. E., Saunders, T. J., Larouche, R., Colley, R. C., & Gorber, S. C. (2011). Systematic review of sedentary behaviour and health indicators in school-aged children and youth. *Int J Behav Nutr Phys Act, 8*(1), 98.

Tripp, A., French, R., & Sherrill, C. (1995). Contact theory and attitudes of children in physical education programs toward peers with disabilities. *Adapted physical activity quarterly, 12*, 323-323.

Tsiros, M. D., Coates, A. M., Howe, P. R., Walkley, J., Hills, A. P., Wood, R. E., & Buckley, J. D. (2014). Are obese children really less fit? Influences of body composition and physical activity on cardiorespiratory fitness in obese and healthy-weight children. *Obesity Research & Clinical Practice, 8*, 106.

Turner III, D. W. (2010). Qualitative interview design: A practical guide for novice investigators. *The qualitative report, 15*(3), 754.

Turner, L., Chaloupka, F. J., Chriqui, J. F., & Sandoval, A. (2010). School policies and practices to improve health and prevent obesity: National elementary school survey results: School years 2006-07 and 2007-08. *Health Policy Center, Institute for Health Research and Policy, University of Illinois at Chicago.*

Tyrer, F., McGrother, C. W., Thorp, C. F., Donaldson, M., Bhaumik, S., Watson, J. M., & Hollin, C. (2006). Physical aggression towards others in adults with learning disabilities: prevalence and associated factors. *Journal of Intellectual Disability Research, 50*(4), 295- 304.

Ulstad, S. O., Halvari, H., Sørebø, Ø., & Deci, E. L. (2016). Motivation, Learning Strategies, and Performance in Physical Education at Secondary School. *Advances in Physical Education, 6*(01), 27.

Umhoefer, D. L., Vargas, T. M., & Beyer, R. (2015). Adapted Physical Education Service Approaches and the Effects on the Perceived Efficacy Beliefs of General Physical Education Teachers. *Physical Educator, 72*(3), 361.

University of Miami. (2016). Collecting and analyzing interview data. Retrieved from http://yyy.rsmas.miami.edu

University of Wisconsin. (2014). *Data collection method.* Retrieved from http://people.uwec.edu/piercech/researchmethods/data

US News and World Report. (2013). [Name] campus high school overview. Retrieved from https://www.usnews.com//districts/

U.S. Census Bureau. (2010). Housing characteristics. http://factfinder.census.gov/faces/tableservices/jsf/pages/productview.xhtml?src=bkmk

U.S. Census Bureau. (2013). More than 50 million Americans report some level of disability. Retrieved from http://www.census.gov/Press- Release/www/releases/archives/aging population/006809.html

U. S. Department of Education. (nd). Office of Special Education and Rehabilitative Services. History: Twenty-Five Years of Progress in Educating Children With Disabilities Through IDEA. Retrieved from http://www.ed.gov/policy/speced/leg/idea/history.pdf

U. S. Department of Education (2004). Building the legacy 2004. Retrieved from http://idea.ed.gov/explore/view/p/,root,statute

U.S. Department of Education. (2016). How many students with disabilities are in schools? Retrieved from http://www.data-first.org/data/how-many-students-with-disabilities-in-our-schools/

U.S. Department of Education. (2016). Office of Elementary and Secondary Education. Retrieved from www2.ed.gov/about/offices/list/oese/index.html

U. S. Department of Health and Human Services. (2008). Centers for Disease Control and Prevention. Healthy children and adults. Retrieved from http://www.cdc.gov/healthyschools/health

U. S. Department of Health and Human Services. (2010). Centers for Disease Control and Prevention. The association between school based physical activity and academic performance. Retrieved from http://www.cdc.gov/healthyschools/health_and_academics/pdf/pa-pe_paper.pdf

U. S. Department of Health and Human Services. (2010). Let's move! Retrieved from http://www.letsmove.gov

U.S. Government Accountability Office. (2010). Students with disabilities, More information and guidance could improve opportunities in physical education and athletics. Highlights of GAO-10-519, a report to congressional requesters. Retrieved from http://www.gao.gov/assets/310/305770.pdf

U.S. Government Accountability Office. (2011). *Students with disabilities: More information and guidance could improve opportunities in physical education and athletics* (GAO-10- 519). Retrieved from http://www.gao.gov/new.items/d10519.pdf

Vaillo, R. R., Hutzler, Y., Santiago, M. C. I., & Murcia, J. A. M. (2016). Attitudes towards Inclusion of Students with Disabilities in Physical Education Questionnaire (AISDPE): A two-component scale in Spanish. *European Journal of Human Movement, 36,* 75-87.

Van den Berghe, L., Vansteenkiste, M., Cardon, G., Kirk, D., & Haerens, L. (2014). Research on self-determination in physical education: Key findings and proposals for future research. *Physical Education and Sport Pedagogy, 19*(1), 97-121.

Van Teijlingen, E. (2014). Semi-structured interviews. Revived from https://intranetsp.bournemouth.ac.uk

Van Vugt, E. S., Deković, M., Prinzie, P., Stams, G. J. J. M., & Asscher, J. J. (2013). Evaluation of a group-based social skills training for children with problem behavior. *Children and Youth Services Review, 35*(1), 162-167.

Van Wely, L., Balemans, A. C., Becher, J. G., & Dallmeijer, A. J. (2014). The effectiveness of a physical activity stimulation programme for children with cerebral palsy on social participation, self-perception and quality of life: a randomized controlled trial. *Clinical rehabilitation, 28*(10), 972-982.

Verret, C., Guay, M. C., Berthiaume, C., Gardiner, P., & Béliveau, L. (2010). A physical activity program improves behaviour and cognitive functions in children with ADHD: An exploratory study. *Journal of Attention Disorders.*

Vertinsky, P. (2012). Reclaiming space, revisioning the body: the quest for gender sensitive physical education. *Taylor & Francis online.* 373-396

Wang, L., Wang, M., & Wen, H. (2015). Teaching Practice of Physical Education Teachers for Students with Special Needs: An Application of the Theory of Planned Behaviour. *International Journal of Disability, Development and Education, 62*(6), 590-607.

Wang, L., Qi, J., & Wang, L. (2015). Beliefs of Chinese physical educators on teaching students with disabilities in general physical education classes. *Adapted Physical Activity Quarterly, 32*(2).

Wang, Y. C., McPherson, K., Marsh, T., Gortmaker, S. L., & Brown, M. (2011). Health and economic burden of the projected obesity trends in the USA and the UK. *The Lancet, 378*(9793), 815-825.

Wang, Y., Li, M., Dong, F., Zhang, J., & Zhang, F. (2015). Physical exercise-induced protection on ischemic cardiovascular and cerebrovascular diseases. *International journal of clinical and experimental medicine, 8*(11), 19859.

Waters, E., de Silva-Sanigorski, A., Hall, B. J., Brown, T., Campbell, K. J., Gao, Y., & Summerbell, C. D. (2011). Interventions for preventing obesity in children. *Cochrane Database Syst Rev, 12*(00).

Webster-Stratton, C. (2015). THE INCREDIBLE YEARS® SERIES. *Family-Based Prevention Programs for Children and Adolescents: Theory, Research, and Large-Scale Dissemination, 42.*

Weiser, B. (2014). Academic diversity: ways to motivate and engage students with learning disabilities. *Council for learning disability journal.* Retrieved from http://www.council- for-learning-disabilities.org/wp-content/uploads/2014/07/Weiser_Motivation.pdf

Wen, C. P., Wai, J. P. M., Tsai, M. K., Yang, Y. C., Cheng, T. Y. D., Lee, M. C., & Wu, X. (2011). Minimum amount of physical activity for reduced mortality and extended life expectancy: a prospective cohort study. *The Lancet, 378*(9798), 1244-1253.

Wentzel, K. (2012). Part III commentary: Socio-cultural contexts, social competence, and engagement at school. In *Handbook of research on student engagement* (pp. 479-488). Springer US.

Werner, S., Corrigan, P., Ditchman, N., & Sokol, K. (2012). Stigma and intellectual disability: A review of related measures and future directions. *Research in Developmental Disabilities, 33*(2), 748-765.

Wery, J., & Thomson, M. M. (2013). Motivational strategies to enhance effective learning in teaching struggling students. *Support for Learning, 28*(3), 103-108.

Winnick, J., & Porretta, D. (Eds.). (2016). *Adapted Physical Education and Sport, 6E.* Human Kinetics.

Winnick, J. P. (2011). *Adapted physical education and sport.* Human Kinetics.

Woodmansee, C., Hahne, A., Imms, C., & Shields, N. (2016). Comparing participation in physical recreation activities between children with disability and children with typical development: A secondary analysis of matched data. *Research in developmental disabilities, 49,* 268-276.

World Health Organization. (2016). Disabilities. *Better health for people with disabilities.* Retrieved from http://www.who.int/topics/disabilities/en/

World Health Organization. (2016). Health education. Retrieved from http://www.who.int/topics/health_education/en/

Wright, N., & Stickley, T. (2013). Concepts of social inclusion, exclusion and mental health: a review of the international literature. *Journal of psychiatric and mental health nursing, 20*(1), 71-81.

Wu, H. T., Chou, M. J., Chen, W. H., & Tu, C. T. (2016). Relationship among Family Support, Love Attitude, and Well-Being of Junior High School Students. *Universal Journal of Educational Research, 4*(2), 370-377.

Yin, R. K. (2011). *Applications of case study research.* Sage.

Yin, R. K. (2013). *Case study research: Design and methods.* Sage publications.

Yin, Z., Moore, J. B., Johnson, M. H., Vernon, M. M., & Gutin, B. (2012). The impact of a 3- year after-school obesity prevention program in elementary school children. *Childhood obesity, 8*(1), 60-70.

Yli-Piipari, S., Watt, A., Jaakkola, T., Liukkonen, J., & Nurmi, J. E. (2009). Relationships between physical education students' motivational profiles, enjoyment, state anxiety, and self-reported physical activity. *Journal of Sports Science and Medicine, 8*(3), 327-336.

Ziviani, J., Poulsen, A., & Cuskelly, M. (Eds.). (2012). *The art and science of motivation: A therapist's guide to working with children.* Jessica Kingsley Publishers.

Zhang, D., Katsiyannis, A., Ju, S., & Roberts, E. (2014). Minority representation in special education: 5-year trends. *Journal of Child and Family Studies, 23*(1), 118-127.

Zhang, J., Piwowar, N., & Reilly, C. J. (2009). Physical fitness performance of young adults with and without cognitive impairments. *Journal of International Council for Health, Physical Education, Recreations, Sport, and Dance, 4*(1), 46

APPENDICES

Appendix A

Annotated Bibliography

Abdi, E. (2015). 'Theoretical Literature Review on Lack of Cardiorespiratory Fitness and Its Effects on Children'. *World Academy of Science, Engineering and Technology, International Science Index* 103, 9(7).

The purpose of this theoretical literature review was to study the relevant academic literature on lack of cardiorespiratory fitness and its effects on children. The researcher identified total of thirty eight relevant documents and considered for the review. Nineteen of those articles were original research articles published in peer reviewed journals and the other nineteen were statistical documents. The literature review was structured to examine 5 effects in deficiency of cardiorespiratory fitness in school aged children (A) Relative Age Effect (RAE), (B) Obesity, (C) Inadequate fitness level (D) Unhealthy life style, and (E) Academics. The categories provided a theoretical framework for future studies where results were driven from the literature review. The study discussed that regular physical fitness assists children and adolescents to develop healthy physical activity behaviors which can be sustained throughout adult life. Conclusion suggested that advocacy for increasing physical activity and decreasing sedentary behaviors at school and home are necessary.

Bernstein, E., Phillips, S. R., & Silverman, S. (2011). Attitudes and perceptions of middle school students toward competitive activities in physical education. *Journal of teaching in physical education*, *30*(1), 69-83.

In this study researchers examined the attitudes and perceptions of middle school students toward competitive activities in physical education. The sample was composed of 6 schools with ten boys and 14 girls volunteered with 11-high-skilled, 11 moderate-skilled, and 2 low skilled students in 6th and 7th grades. All students were in competitive activities. Data collection included focus groups consist of students with mixed skill levels, observations of competitive class activities, and informal interviews with teachers conducted over several months. The researchers concluded the three major themes emerged from the study, 1) having fun in competitive activities, 2) not all students were attaining motor skills necessary to participate in activities due to a lack of time to engage in appropriate practice, and 3) the structure of competitive activities affects student experience.

Boddy, L. M., Downs, S. J., Knowles, Z. R., & Fairclough, S. J. (2015). Physical activity and play behaviours in children and young people with intellectual disabilities: A cross-sectional observational study. *School Psychology International, 36*(2), 154-171.

The researchers start with well-established benefits of physical activity and active play for children and young people however it is stated that there is a lack of physical activity research involving children and young people with intellectual disabilities. Seventy participants between ages of 5 to 15 with intellectual disabilities were investigated. Routine physical activity and recess play behavior using objective methods of accelerometers and systematic observation techniques were examined. According h the observation most of the participants recess time was spent alone or playing in small groups, with no participants engaging in large group play. However older participants spent more recess time playing in small groups rather than playing alone. There was a positive correlations between time spent alone and physical activity. Results specified that few children were active enough to benefit their physical health. No differences in routine physical activity, sedentary behavior, or recess play behaviors were observed between boys and girls. Authors showed that these findings contrast with those typically observed in a mainstream school setting. While implications for school psychologists were discussed, in conclusion researchers suggested that interventions designed from formative research are needed to promote physical activity within this population.

Clapham, E. D., & Lamont, L. S. (2015, March). Catching Waves for Health: Exploring the Benefits of Surfing. In *Research Quarterly for Exercise and Sport* (vol. 86, pp. a12- a12). 4 Park Square, Milton Park, Abingdon ox14 4rn, Oxfordshire, England: Routledge Journals, Taylor & Francis Ltd.

For this 8 week program twenty-nine children ages 5-18 years, from the University of Rhode Island Adapted Physical Education Program, Special Olympics Rhode Island and through word-of-mouth were selected and pre/ post-testing measurements were used. The purpose of this study was to assess the effectiveness of a surfing intervention on the strength, flexibility, cardiorespiratory endurance, amount of activity, balance, range of motion, bone density, and at the end program evaluation of children with disabilities. Therefore the study attained to examine that lack of fitness and recreation opportunities for children with disabilities is problematic. This can be substantial to proper health development. According to researchers children with disabilities can benefit more from adapted aquatics in terms of necessary physical activity and educational programming than for their non-disabled peers. This applies to surfing in the ocean as well. Brockport Physical Fitness Test (BPFT) was used and scan measurements were recorded. Each hour surf lesson included paddle in the water, balance on board, and ride a wave on the board progressing from laying, to kneeling, to standing. The analysis results were discovering improvements in endurance ($P < 0.015$) and cardiorespiratory endurance (20-m) PACER ($P < 0.047$). Researchers concluded that there is an overall improvement in upper body strength and cardiorespiratory endurance in these participants. Physiological effectiveness of surfing for children with disabilities were suggested for further research.

Collins, R. (2012). *Attitudes of middle school students with disabilities toward physical education: a mixed methods examination.* Northcentral University.

In this study Collins pinpointed that students with disabilities engage in significantly less physical activity than their nondisabled peers due to their attitudes. Continues of participation in physical activities can be influenced by aptitude. Collins found the gap in the literature with respect to examining the attitudes of students with high incidence disabilities such as learning disabilities, emotional/ behavioral disabilities, or attention difficulties. The purpose of this mixed methods study was to establish the degree to which differences in attitude toward physical education exist between groups of students. Therefore middle school students with and without high incidence disabilities were selected to investigate their insights and experiences in hopes to define factors that influence their attitudes. There were two phases involved in this study, in Phase 1, quantitative data were collected through a survey of 134 randomly selected middle school students with and without disabilities attending public schools in northern Wisconsin. Analytic results used descriptive statistics and the Mann-Whitney U Test. There was no statistically significant differences noticeable in enjoyment (Z = -.958, p = .338) or perceived usefulness (Z = -1.667, p = .096) of physical education between students with and without disabilities. Twenty one participants were selected in phase 2 which shared their experiences and insights during personal interviews. This quantitative phase shared to help explain and expand upon data obtained. Student Attitude Towards Physical Activity Scale (SATPES) was used for interview data. Answered were examined for similarities and differences influencing attitudes toward physical education and activity between students with and without disabilities with very high and very low scores. An analysis of interview data revealed more similarities between students with and without disabilities than differences. The researcher noticed that teachers have control over factors influencing student attitudes toward physical education. The study was concluded with improving student attitudes which may result in continued participation in physical activity. Increased academic performance and improved physical and mental health for all students was also noted.

Dismore, H., & Bailey, R. (2010). 'It's been a bit of a rocky start': attitudes toward physical education following transition. *Physical Education and Sport Pedagogy*, *15*(2), 175-191.

Researchers implied that previous studies have identified a number of factors that exist to influence attitudes toward physical education, but little research has focused upon the transition between Key Stages (KS) when many children transfer from primary to secondary schools. This study presented data related to the attitudes of children and young people toward physical education, and specifically to their transition from (7–11 year olds) to (11–14 year olds). Participants were chosen from schools in a borough located in the south-east of England which represented a range of school types. Data were collected on their feelings and beliefs toward physical education using individual interviews with 10 children after they had been transferred. The results showed that students' attitudes remained consistent across the transition and there were few differences between the attitudes of those attending primary/secondary schools and middle schools. After all many of these children expressed positive attitudes toward physical education however certain patterns emerged in relation to how other structures and processes influenced children. Attitudes toward physical education were generally described in terms for fun and enjoyment to social relations and the physical education facilities. Children discussed progressing from having fun to experiencing a serious skills-based curriculum in physical education. In conclusion the study illustrated the complexities of children's attitudes following the transition. In particular, 2 issues were raised one, the consequences of pupils adopting the values of a 'performative culture' within physical education; second, the important role physical education plays within the curriculum, particularly as a setting for social development.

Gaddes, W. H. (2013). *Learning disabilities and brain function: A neuropsychological approach.* Springer Science & Business Media.

In this book, the author collected the work of other authors and added a completely new chapter on Attention Deficit Disorder (ADD) to the new edition. The puzzle of human leaning, especially academic learning is examined through articles. In the new chapter, students who despite apparently normal intelligence and opportunity, have varying degrees of difficulty in acquiring ideas and skills which are easily mastered by others are discussed. Author indicated that until about fifty years ago there was a common leaning to associate academic success with intelligence. In that view those students who could not meet the demands of the arranged program were usually required to repeat the same grade. This caused the repetition of the same discouraging treatment that was unsuccessful previously.

Grondhuis, S. N., & Aman, M. G. (2014). Overweight and obesity in youth with developmental disabilities: a call to action. *Journal of Intellectual Disability Research, 58*(9), 787- 799.

Regardless of the presence or lack of disability, raising weight status has become primarily a problem for adults and children around the world. In recent decades, youth with intellectual and developmental disabilities are more vulnerable to weight gain in higher rate than mainstream population. There are many circumstances around young people with disabilities which increase their risk for greater body mass. These circumstances include medication use, having syndromes with obesity as an associated symptom, and possessing altered eating habits related to their disability. The researchers discussed obesity related health risks with possible weight management options. Further research is recommended for weight maintenance or loss. It is denoted that most professionals who work with developmental disabled youth do not have great expertise in nutrition and weight management. Therefore collectively recognize the importance of weight issues for quality of life of these individuals is essential. In conclusion one aim of educators should be teaching maintaining healthy lifestyles with intervention options, both for caregivers and for health professionals.

Harvey, W. J., Reid, G., Bloom, G. A., Staples, K., Grizenko, N., Mbekou, V., & Joober, R. (2009). Physical activity experiences of boys with and without ADHD. *Adapted Physical Activity Quarterly, 26*(2), 131.

In this research, physical activity experiences of 12 age-matched boys with and without attention-deficit hyperactivity disorder (ADHD) were explored. Test of Gross Motor Development-2 assessments and semi structured interviews were conducted to covey the information. The knowledge-based approach and the inhibitory model of executive functions emerged during interviews. Skill assessments indicated of students with ADHD were not as proficient movers as their peers without ADHD. Concluded results exposed that boys with ADHD reported however they played with friends but paid little attention to detail, possessed superficial knowledge about movement skills, and expressed many negative feelings about physical activity. Future research in task-specific interventions and a wider range of mixed methods research are recommended for studies in ADHD.

Hutchinson, N., Minnes, P., Burbidge, J., Dods, J., Pyle, A., & Dalton, C. J. (2015). Perspectives of Canadian Teacher Candidates on Inclusion of Children with Developmental Disabilities: A Mixed-Methods Study. *Exceptionality Education International, 25*(2).

The perspectives of 208 teachers on teaching children with developmental disabilities and delays (DD) in inclusive classrooms from Kindergarten to Grade 6 are examined in this mixed method study. A questionnaire with open-ended questions was given to teachers included items on demographics, experience, knowledge, and feelings of competence, advocacy, and sense of efficacy. Outcome suggested that qualitative items produced more positive responses than traditional questionnaire. Also in qualitative data, answers showed understanding of problems associated with inclusive education. Capability of teaching children with DD and collaborating with colleagues predicted general sense of effective scores. Those teachers who were experienced advocating for individuals with disabilities reported greater knowledge, experience, and confidence which were highly correlated to teaching students with DD.

Ickes, M. J., & Sharma, M. (2011). A review of childhood obesity prevention interventions targeting African American children. *Vulnerable Children and Youth Studies, 6*(2), 103-123.

Obesity affects minority youth populations disproportionately, with African Americans (AAs) 1.4 times as likely to be obese as non-Hispanic whites and makes it a significant public health concern. Major roles in the development of obesity in this population are genetic factors, cultural differences related to the nutritional habits, level of physical activity and acceptance of surplus weight among AAs. Researchers indicated that The Institute of Medicine has expressed an urgent need to initiate childhood obesity interventions among diverse ethnic groups. As a result, the purpose of this article was to review existing childhood obesity prevention interventions targeting AA children that were published between 2005 and 2010. The review considered interventions in which the population included more than 35% of AA children and adolescents. Eighteen interventions had been summarized in this review, including behavioral, social and environmental approaches. Recommendations were presented to improve childhood obesity interventions among not only AA rather diverse ethnic groups.

Kelly, S. A., Melnyk, B. M., Jacobson, D. L., & O'Haver, J. A. (2011). Correlates among healthy lifestyle cognitive beliefs, healthy lifestyle choices, social support, and healthy behaviors in adolescents: implications for behavioral change strategies and future research. *Journal of pediatric health care, 25*(4), 216-223.

The purpose of this research was to evaluate the relationships among cognitive variables, social support, and healthy lifestyle behaviors in adolescents. The study indicated that the foundation for healthy lifestyle behaviors begins in childhood. As result, the relationships among cognitive beliefs, healthy lifestyle choices, and healthy lifestyle behaviors in adolescents were explored. The method of this study was a descriptive correlational design with students selected from two high schools in the Southwest United States to participate. The data results showed that significant correlations existed among cognitive variables, social support, behavioral skills, and health lifestyle behaviors. Interestingly, the study established the fact that cognitive beliefs on leading a healthy lifestyle, comprising of attitudes and intentional choices, are related to physical activity as well as the intake of fruits and vegetables. Researchers suggested that in working with adolescents on healthy lifestyle behavior change, strategies have to remain strong on their cognitive beliefs about their ability to make healthy choices and engage in healthy lifestyle behaviors. Reinforcement of these beliefs would demolish the idea that these behaviors are difficult to perform and ultimately should result in healthy behaviors.

Kjønniksen, L., Fjørtoft, I., & Wold, B. (2009). Attitude to physical education and participation in organized youth sports during adolescence related to physical activity in young adulthood: A 10-year longitudinal study. *European Physical Education Review, 15*(2), 139-154.

The purpose of this study was to examine the relationship between participation in organized youth sport and attitude to physical education (PE) during adolescence and physical activity in young adulthood. Six hundred thirty participants were taken as sample and completed questionnaires over a 10-year period. The relationship between attitude to PE and participation in organized sport at age 13 years and physical activity at age 23 years were used to analyze variances and regressions. Both genders were consistent and positive in attitude toward PE at age 13—16 years however more boys participated in organized youth sport, but participation rates declined from age 13 to 16 years. The results comprised that males' participation in organized sport was the strongest predictor of physical activity at age 23 years, whereas attitude to PE for females was the strongest predictor. It was concluded that participation differently in young adult men and women may determine participation in sport and physical activity in different arenas during adolescence.

Lai, S. K., Costigan, S. A., Morgan, P. J., Lubans, D. R., Stodden, D. F., Salmon, J., & Barnett, L. M. (2014). Do school-based interventions focusing on physical activity, fitness, or fundamental movement skill competency produce a sustained impact in these outcomes in children and adolescents? A systematic review of follow up studies. *Sports Medicine, 44*(1), 67-79.

This study was directed by a systematic review to determine if children and adolescents (aged 3–18 years) who have participated in school based interventions have sustained outcomes in Physical Activities (PA), fitness and /or Functional Movement Systems (FMS). Comprised studies were school-based studies including randomized controlled trials, longitudinal cohort, quasi-experimental, and experimental. The methodology used a systematic search of six electronic databases (CINAHL Plus with Full Text, Ovid MEDLINE, SPORTDiscus™, Scopus, PsycINFO and ERIC) which was conducted from 1995 to 26 July 2012. The bias assessment risk was directed by the "Preferred Reporting Items for Systematic Reviews and Meta-Analyses" statement. Fourteen articles were identified by researchers and some studies addressed multiple outcomes: 13 articles assessed PA and ten of those studies reported PA behavior change maintenance. Researchers concluded that it was likely that PA was a sustainable outcome from interventions in children and adolescents. The evidence suggested that interventions of longer than 1 year which utilized a theoretical model or framework were effective in producing the sustained impact. Based on this study it was apparent that FMS were a sustainable outcome in children and adolescents. The authors indicated that the finding need to be viewed with caution given the lack of studies and the risk of bias assessment however more research is needed to assess the sustainability of fitness interventions. Researchers continued to say that this review only included a handful of studies that addressed fitness and only one of these studies found a prolonged impact.

Lotan, M., Hadash, R., Amrani, S., Pinsker, A., & Weiss, T. P. (2015). Improving balance of individuals with intellectual and developmental disability through a virtual reality intervention program. *Palaestra, 29*(4).

The aim of this study was to test the effectiveness of a Virtual Reality (VR) based exercise program in improving the balance of Individual and Development Disability (IDD). The VR technology was investigated for providing a motivating physical fitness program. IDDs are in need of effective physical fitness training programs. Twenty four participants with IDD and balance problems were randomly selected for an eight-week program consisting of two 30-minute sessions per week. The program was implemented through game-like exercises provided by the SeeMe video capture VR system. The researchers reported that significant improvements in balance were demonstrated for the research group in comparison to the control group for the TUG test (Using the two tailed student T-test). The conclusions: of study provided information that VR technology is suitable as a means to improve balance.

Mercier, K., Phillips, S., & Silverman, S. (2016). High School Physical Education Teachers' Attitudes and use of Fitness Tests. *The High School Journal, 99*(2), 179- 190.

The purpose of this study was to understand how fitness tests are used in secondary physical education classes in addition to how the attitudes of physical education teachers toward fitness testing relate to their use of fitness tests. The researchers recapped that recommendations for using and implementing fitness tests have been extensively researched but teachers' attitudes toward fitness tests are beginning to be studied. Therefore less is understood on how high school teachers use fitness tests and the role their attitudes toward fitness tests affect students' attitudes toward physical activity. A sample of 149 high school physical education teachers from 47 school districts completed the Physical Education Teacher Attitudes toward Fitness Tests Scale (PETAFTS). It is a16-item survey on teachers' attitudes toward fitness tests, with additional items on how fitness tests are used. Results designated that teachers often do not implement fitness tests as suggested. Outcome implies that teachers with positive and negative attitudes toward fitness testing fluctuate in their implementation of fitness tests. The use of fitness concept test was more frequent with teachers who had more positive attitudes and the test results were sent home by teachers who thought the implantation of fitness testing was important.

Nelson, T. D., Benson, E. R., & Jensen, C. D. (2010). Negative attitudes toward physical activity: Measurement and role in predicting physical activity levels among preadolescents. *Journal of pediatric psychology, 35*(1), 89-98.

The purpose of this study was to describe the development and validation of a measure of negative attitudes toward physical activity and examine the association between these attitudes and self-reported physical activity among pre adolescents. The sample of this study was school based of 382 fifth and sixth graders who completed measures of attitudes toward physical activity and self-reported physical activity. As a part of a standard school health assessment body mass index data for the participants was collected. The results sustained a significant association between negative attitudes and physical activity. The focus of previous research in this area shows negative attitudes to be a stronger predictor of physical activity than positive attitudes. Researchers had found the same results. The conclusion suggest that negative attitudes toward physical activity can be dependably measured and possibly an important target for intervention efforts to increase physical activity among children and adolescents.

Ogden, C. L., Carroll, M. D., Kit, B. K., & Flegal, K. M. (2014). Prevalence of childhood and adult obesity in the United States, 2011-2012. *Jama*, *311*(8), 806-814.

This study provided the most recent national estimates and analyze trends in childhood obesity between 2003 and 2012 in addition to offering detailed obesity trend analyses among adults. Weight and height or resting length were measured in 9120 participants in the 2011-2012 nationally representative National Health and Nutrition Examination Survey. The outcome results indicated that overall, there was no significant change from 2003-2004 through 2011-2012 in high weight for recumbent length among infants and toddlers and obesity in 2- to 19-year-olds, or obesity in adults. However there was a significant decrease in obesity among 2- to 5-year-old children (from 13.9% to 8.4%; $P = .03$) and a significant increase in obesity among women aged 60 years and older (from 31.5% to 38.1%; $P = .006$). The researchers concluded that there have been no significant changes in obesity prevalence in youth or adults between 2003-2004 and 2011-2012. Obesity prevalence remains high and as a result it is important to continue the investigation.

Singh, G. K., Kogan, M. D., & Van Dyck, P. C. (2010). Changes in state-specific childhood obesity and overweight prevalence in the United States from 2003 to 2007. *Archives of pediatrics & adolescent medicine*, *164*(7), 598-607.

In this study researchers examined changes in state specific obesity and overweight prevalence among US children and adolescents between 2003 and 2007. The 50 states and District of Columbia were part of the setting for this research. A Temporal cross-sectional analysis of the 2003 and 2007 National Survey of Children's Health data was set as a design.

Participants were a total of 46, 707 and 44, 101 children aged 10 to 17 years in 2003 and 2007. Differentials in prevalence and odds of obesity and overweight were examined by bivariate and logistic regression analyses. The researchers reported that in 2007, 16.4% of US children were obese and 31.6% were overweight. The prevalence of obesity varied substantially across the states. Respectively individual, household, and neighborhood social and built environmental characteristics accounted for 45% and 42% of the state variance in childhood obesity. Extensive geographic differences in childhood obesity and overweight exist, with an apparent shift toward higher prevalence in 2007 for several states concluded the study.

Smith, G. A. (2012). Perceptions and evaluation of a physical activity program. ProQuest Dissertations & Theses Global. (1277537719). Retrieved from http://search.proquest.com.proxy1.ncu.edu/docview/1277537719

This qualitative case study was conducted in the Midwest of United States to explore the Perceptions of teachers at two different elementary schools as they implemented a physical activity program during the school day. This program engaged students in daily Physical exercise. Six primary themes were uncovered by interviews and classroom observations. There were differences between urban-suburban schools, primary-intermediate grades, gender, teacher participation and enthusiasm, relationships to other lessons, variety in music selections, student leadership, and combining singing or chanting with physical activity. A deeper understanding of program implementation was gained through these themes, and the researcher recommended future implementation.

Standage, M., Gillison, F. B., Ntoumanis, N., & Treasure, D. C. (2012). Predicting students' physical activity and health-related well-being: A prospective cross-domain investigation of motivation across school physical education and exercise settings. *Journal of Sport & Exercise Psychology, 2012*(34), 37-60.

A model of motivation guided by self-determination theory, spanning the contexts of school physical education (PE) and exercise was used in a three-wave prospective design. Health-related quality of life (HRQoL), physical self-concept (PSC), and 4 days of objectively assessed estimates of activity were examined in outcome variables. The sample was consist of 494 secondary school students who completed questionnaires at three separate time points. The students were familiarized with how to use a sealed pedometer. Perceptions of autonomy support from a PE teacher positively predicted PE-related need satisfaction which included autonomy, competence, and relatedness, therefore structural equation modeling supported its model. Autonomy and competence positively predicted motivation toward PE whereas competence also predicted PSC which positively predicted motivation toward exercise such as a 4-day pedometer step count. The results of study was that multi-sample structural equation modeling supported gender invariance. Researchers strongly suggested future work in this area.

Strean, W. B. (2009). Remembering instructors: Play, pain and pedagogy. *Qualitative research in sport and exercise, 1*(3), 210-220.

Contribution in making sport and physical education more fun for children was undertaken in this study. Coaches and teachers were examined on how physical education programs operate in terms of enjoyment. Twenty-four reflective accounts resulted in five major themes: (1) personal characteristics of instructors/coaches, (2) learning environments, (3) peak moments in low-organized activities, (4) social aspects, and (5) lessons from negative experiences. Results were reflected in discussion in relation to fun, enjoyment and happiness in youth sport and physical education.

Subramaniam, P. R., & Silverman, S. (2007). Middle school students' attitudes toward physical education. *Teaching and Teacher Education, 23*(5), 602-611.

Researchers' purpose of this study was to determine middle school students' attitudes toward physical education using an attitude instrument grounded in attitude theory. Furthermore, this investigation also pursued to determine if gender and grade level influence student attitudes toward the subject matter. Participants selected for this study were 995 students from grades 6 to 8. Generally, all students had moderately positive attitudes toward physical education however a decline in attitude was observed as students progressed in grade level.

Van Wely, L., Balemans, A. C., Becher, J. G., & Dallmeijer, A. J. (2014). The effectiveness of a physical activity stimulation programme for children with cerebral palsy on social participation, self-perception and quality of life: a randomized controlled trial. *Clinical rehabilitation, 28*(10), 972-982.

The purpose of this study was to determine the effects of a six-month physical activity stimulation program on social participation, self-perception and quality of life in children with cerebral palsy. Forty-nine children with spastic cerebral palsy (28 male), aged 7–13 years, able to walk with and without walking aids were selected as participants. The intervention group followed a six-month physical activity stimulation program which was involved through counselling with motivational interviewing, home-based physiotherapy and four months of fitness training. The control group continued regular physiotherapy. Results in intervention was in a positive effect on social participation in domestic life at twelve months but not at six months. Researchers reported that no significant effects were found for social participation in recreation and leisure, self-perception at six months and twelve months or for quality of life at twelve months. In conclusions researchers suggested that the combination of counselling, home-based physiotherapy and fitness training was not effective in improving social participation in recreation and leisure, self-perception or quality of life however it did show a potential for improving social participation in domestic life over the longer term.

Wang, Y. C., McPherson, K., Marsh, T., Gortmaker, S. L., & Brown, M. (2011). Health and economic burden of the projected obesity trends in the USA and the UK. *The Lancet, 378*(9793), 815-825.

The raise of several diseases such as cardiovascular diseases, diabetes, and cancers are attributed to frequency of obesity worldwide which makes it a health concern due to excess weight gain within populations. Researchers used a simulation model to develop the apparent health and economic consequences in the next two decades from a continued rise in obesity in two ageing populations. These two countries were the USA and the UK. The trends projected that there will be 65 million more obese adults in the USA and 11 million more obese adults in the UK by 2030. This would cause an additional 6 to 8·5 million cases of diabetes, 5·7 to 7·3 million cases of heart disease and stroke, 492,000 to 669,000 additional cases of cancer while 26 to 55 million quality of life are faded for USA and UK combined. According to researchers by 2030, the medical costs associated with treatment of these avoidable conditions are estimated to increase by $48 to 66 billion a year in the USA and by £1·9 to 2 billion a year in the UK. Authors pointed out that effective policies should be in place to promote healthier weight and also economic benefits.

Zhang, J., Piwowar, N., & Reilly, C. J. (2009). Physical fitness performance of young adults with and without cognitive impairments. *The ICHPER-SD Journal of Research in Health, Physical Education, Recreation, Sport & Dance, 4*(1), 46.

The purpose of this investigation was to analyze the physical fitness performance of young adults with and without cognitive impairments. Participants were Seventy five young adults, including 41 without disabilities and 34 with mild cognitive impairments participated in this study. The Brockport Physical Fitness Test with seven test items including 20-m pacer, curl-ups, flexed arm hang, skinfolds of triceps, skinfolds of calf, sit and reach with left leg, and sit and reach with right leg were selected. Participants with and without cognitive impairments were analyzed on physical fitness test items with multivariable analysis. The results revealed a significant difference between two groups. These findings implied that young adults with cognitive impairments showed lower fitness performance on cardiovascular endurance, muscular strength and endurance, and range of motion than their normal peers.

Appendix B
Recruitment Letter

Dear [Name],

Appendix C

Letter to principals

Appendix D

Interview Guide

General introductory interview questions:

What grades do you teach this year?
How many students with learning disabilities are you teaching?
Do you teach self-contain, inclusion or both classes?
How many years have you been teaching?
How many years are you teaching at this district?
How many years have you been teaching in this school?

Open-ended interview questions:

1. When students with learning disabilities **enjoyed** participating in physical education class:
   a.) What did you do to make the activities enjoyable as a physical education teacher?
   b.) What roles did students with learning disabilities play in the gymnasium?
   c.) What roles did students without learning disabilities (if an inclusion class) play in the gymnasium?
   d.) What roles did individual skill level play in successful activities?
   e.) How unstructured were the activities?

2. When students with learning disabilities **did not enjoy** participating in physical education class:
   a.) What role did you play as a physical education teacher?

b.) What roles did students with learning disabilities play in the gymnasium?

c.) What roles did students without learning disabilities (if an inclusion class) play in the gymnasium?

d.) What roles did individual skill levels play in successful activities?

e.) How unstructured were the activities?

3. When you thought the activities are **useful** for students with learning disabilities in physical education class:

a.) As a physical education teacher, what did you do to make the activities useful?

b.) What roles did students with learning disabilities play in the gymnasium?

c.) What roles did students without learning disabilities (if an inclusion class) play in the gymnasium?

d.) What roles did individual skill level play in successful activities?

e.) How unstructured were the activities?

4. When you thought the activities are **not useful** for students with learning disabilities in physical education class:

a.) What role did you play as a physical education teacher?

b.) What roles did students with learning disabilities play in the gymnasium?

c.) What roles did students without learning disabilities (if an inclusion class) play the gymnasium?

d.) What roles did individual skill level play in successful activities?

e.) How unstructured were the activities?

5. If you could change one thing to make physical education more **enjoyable** for students with learning disabilities, what would it be?

6. If you could change one thing to make physical education more **usefulness** for students with learning disabilities, what would it be?

7. In order to increase positive attitude and behavior of students with learning disabilities in physical education:

a.) Should students participate in self-contained physical education which means more restricted environment?

b.) Should students participate in non-co-ed physical education classes?

8. Do you think children with learning disabilities suffer from lack of physical activity during your physical education class? If yes:
    a.) What are the factors related to lack of physical activity for students with learning disabilities?

9. What are your suggestions in helping students with learning disabilities to increase physical activity in physical education class?

10. What are your experiences in helping students with learning disabilities to improve their attitude in physical education participation?

About the Author

Internationally recognized expert in education Dr. Ellie Abdi is a former gymnast, dancer and coach whom has held many academic roles from PK to doctoral level and currently at two American and two French Universities plus a school district. Dr. Abdi was an elected VP of physical education in New Jersey and an elect-chair of Diversity for SHAPE-America who advocates before the Congress in DC. Professor Abdi is an Editorial Board Member of several International journals in Turkey, India, Bulgaria and United States, a review editor for a Swiss journal and an invitee member of scientific committees at many conferences. A presenter of many papers, keynotes and workshops who has published many research, interviews and articles. She is the author of 2 books on education and contributed several chapters in few books on biomechanics.

Printed in the United States
By Bookmasters